Kâlidâsa, Ralph Thomas Hotchkin Griffith

**The Birth of the War-God**

A Poem

Kâlidâsa, Ralph Thomas Hotchkin Griffith

**The Birth of the War-God**
*A Poem*

ISBN/EAN: 9783337005948

Printed in Europe, USA, Canada, Australia, Japan

Cover: Foto ©Thomas Meinert / pixelio.de

More available books at **www.hansebooks.com**

# TRÜBNER'S ORIENTAL SERIES.

"A knowledge of the commonplace, at least, of Oriental literature, philosophy, and religion is as necessary to the general reader of the present day as an acquaintance with the Latin and Greek classics was a generation or so ago. Immense strides have been made within the present century in these branches of learning; Sanskrit has been brought within the range of accurate philology, and its invaluable ancient literature thoroughly investigated; the language and sacred books of the Zoroastrians have been laid bare; Egyptian, Assyrian, and other records of the remote past have been deciphered, and a group of scholars speak of still more recondite Accadian and Hittite monuments; but the results of all the scholarship that has been devoted to these subjects have been almost inaccessible to the public because they were contained for the most part in learned or expensive works, or scattered throughout the numbers of scientific periodicals. Messrs. TRÜBNER & Co., in a spirit of enterprise which does them infinite credit, have determined to supply the constantly-increasing want, and to give in a popular, or, at least, a comprehensive form, all this mass of knowledge to the world."—*Times.*

---

Second Edition, post 8vo, pp. xxxii.—748, with Map, cloth, price 21s.

## THE INDIAN EMPIRE :
## ITS PEOPLE, HISTORY, AND PRODUCTS.

By the Hon. Sir W. W. HUNTER, K.C.S.I., C.S.I., C.I.E., LL.D.

Member of the Viceroy's Legislative Council,
Director-General of Statistics to the Government of India.

Being a Revised Edition, brought up to date, and incorporating the general results of the Census of 1881.

"It forms a volume of more than 700 pages, and is a marvellous combination of literary condensation and research. It gives a complete account of the Indian Empire, its history, peoples, and products, and forms the worthy outcome of seventeen years of labour with exceptional opportunities for rendering that labour fruitful. Nothing could be more lucid than Sir William Hunter's expositions of the economic and political condition of India at the present time, or more interesting than his scholarly history of the India of the past."—*The Times.*

*THE FOLLOWING WORKS HAVE ALREADY APPEARED:—*

Third Edition, post 8vo, cloth, pp. xvi.—428, price 16s.

## ESSAYS ON THE SACRED LANGUAGE, WRITINGS, AND RELIGION OF THE PARSIS.

BY MARTIN HAUG, PH.D.,

Late of the Universities of Tübingen, Göttingen, and Bonn; Superintendent of Sanskrit Studies, and Professor of Sanskrit in the Poona College.

EDITED AND ENLARGED BY DR. E. W. WEST.

To which is added a Biographical Memoir of the late Dr. HAUG by Prof. E. P. EVANS.

I. History of the Researches into the Sacred Writings and Religion of the Parsis, from the Earliest Times down to the Present.
II. Languages of the Parsi Scriptures.
III. The Zend-Avesta, or the Scripture of the Parsis.
IV. The Zoroastrian Religion, as to its Origin and Development.

"'Essays on the Sacred Language, Writings, and Religion of the Parsis,' by the late Dr. Martin Haug, edited by Dr. E. W. West. The author intended, on his return from India, to expand the materials contained in this work into a comprehensive account of the Zoroastrian religion, but the design was frustrated by his untimely death. We have, however, in a concise and readable form, a history of the researches into the sacred writings and religion of the Parsis from the earliest times down to the present—a dissertation on the languages of the Parsi Scriptures, a translation of the Zend-Avesta, or the Scripture of the Parsis, and a dissertation on the Zoroastrian religion, with especial reference to its origin and development."—*Times.*

Post 8vo, cloth, pp. viii.—176, price 7s. 6d.

## TEXTS FROM THE BUDDHIST CANON

### COMMONLY KNOWN AS "DHAMMAPADA."

*With Accompanying Narratives.*

Translated from the Chinese by S. BEAL, B.A., Professor of Chinese, University College, London.

The Dhammapada, as hitherto known by the Pali Text Edition, as edited by Fausböll, by Max Müller's English, and Albrecht Weber's German translations, consists only of twenty-six chapters or sections, whilst the Chinese version, or rather recension, as now translated by Mr. Beal, consists of thirty-nine sections. The students of Pali who possess Fausböll's text, or either of the above-named translations, will therefore needs want Mr. Beal's English rendering of the Chinese version; the thirteen above-named additional sections not being accessible to them in any other form; for, even if they understand Chinese, the Chinese original would be unobtainable by them.

"Mr. Beal's rendering of the Chinese translation is a most valuable aid to the critical study of the work. It contains authentic texts gathered from ancient canonical books, and generally connected with some incident in the history of Buddha. Their great interest, however, consists in the light which they throw upon everyday life in India at the remote period at which they were written, and upon the method of teaching adopted by the founder of the religion. The method employed was principally parable, and the simplicity of the tales and the excellence of the morals inculcated, as well as the strange hold which they have retained upon the minds of millions of people, make them a very remarkable study."—*Times.*

"Mr. Beal, by making it accessible in an English dress, has added to the great services he has already rendered to the comparative study of religious history."—*Academy.*

"Valuable as exhibiting the doctrine of the Buddhists in its purest, least adulterated form, it brings the modern reader face to face with that simple creed and rule of conduct which won its way over the minds of myriads, and which is now nominally professed by 145 millions, who have overlaid its austere simplicity with innumerable ceremonies, forgotten its maxims, perverted its teaching, and so inverted its leading principle that a religion whose founder denied a God, now worships that founder as a god himself."—*Scotsman.*

Second Edition, post 8vo, cloth, pp. xxiv.—360, price 10s. 6d.

## THE HISTORY OF INDIAN LITERATURE.

### By ALBRECHT WEBER.

Translated from the Second German Edition by JOHN MANN, M.A., and THÉODOR ZACHARIAE, Ph.D., with the sanction of the Author.

Dr. BUHLER, Inspector of Schools in India, writes:—"When I was Professor of Oriental Languages in Elphinstone College, I frequently felt the want of such a work to which I could refer the students."

Professor COWELL, of Cambridge, writes:—"It will be especially useful to the students in our Indian colleges and universities. I used to long for such a book when I was teaching in Calcutta. Hindu students are intensely interested in the history of Sanskrit literature, and this volume will supply them with all they want on the subject."

Professor WHITNEY, Yale College, Newhaven, Conn., U.S.A., writes:—"I was one of the class to whom the work was originally given in the form of academic lectures. At their first appearance they were by far the most learned and able treatment of their subject; and with their recent additions they still maintain decidedly the same rank."

"Is perhaps the most comprehensive and lucid survey of Sanskrit literature extant. The essays contained in the volume were originally delivered as academic lectures, and at the time of their first publication were acknowledged to be by far the most learned and able treatment of the subject. They have now been brought up to date by the addition of all the most important results of recent research."—*Times.*

Post 8vo, cloth, pp. xii.—198, accompanied by Two Language Maps, price 12s.

## A SKETCH OF
## THE MODERN LANGUAGES OF THE EAST INDIES.

### By ROBERT N. CUST.

The Author has attempted to fill up a vacuum, the inconvenience of which pressed itself on his notice. Much had been written about the languages of the East Indies, but the extent of our present knowledge had not even been brought to a focus. It occurred to him that it might be of use to others to publish in an arranged form the notes which he had collected for his own edification.

"Supplies a deficiency which has long been felt."—*Times.*

"The book before us is then a valuable contribution to philological science. It passes under review a vast number of languages, and it gives, or professes to give, in every case the sum and substance of the opinions and judgments of the best-informed writers."—*Saturday Review.*

Second Corrected Edition, post 8vo, pp. xii.—116, cloth, price

## THE BIRTH OF THE WAR-GOD.

### A Poem. By KALIDASA.

Translated from the Sanskrit into English Verse by
RALPH T. H. GRIFFITH, M.A.

"A very spirited rendering of the *Kumárasambhava*, which was first published twenty-six years ago, and which we are glad to see made once more accessible."—*Times.*

"Mr. Griffith's very spirited rendering is well known to most who are at all interested in Indian literature, or enjoy the tenderness of feeling and rich creative imagination of its author."—*Indian Antiquary.*

"We are very glad to welcome a second edition of Professor Griffith's admirable translation. Few translations deserve a second edition better."—*Athenæum.*

Post 8vo, pp. 432, cloth, price 16s.

## A CLASSICAL DICTIONARY OF HINDU MYTHOLOGY AND RELIGION, GEOGRAPHY, HISTORY, AND LITERATURE.

By JOHN DOWSON, M.R.A.S.,
Late Professor of Hindustani, Staff College.

"This not only forms an indispensable book of reference to students of Indian literature, but is also of great general interest, as it gives in a concise and easily accessible form all that need be known about the personages of Hindu mythology whose names are so familiar, but of whom so little is known outside the limited circle of savants."—*Times.*

"It is no slight gain when such subjects are treated fairly and fully in a moderate space; and we need only add that the few wants which we may hope to see supplied in new editions detract but little from the general excellence of Mr. Dowson's work."—*Saturday Review.*

Post 8vo, with View of Mecca, pp. cxii.—172, cloth, price 9s.

## SELECTIONS FROM THE KORAN.

By EDWARD WILLIAM LANE,
Translator of "The Thousand and One Nights;" &c., &c.
A New Edition, Revised and Enlarged, with an Introduction by
STANLEY LANE POOLE.

"... Has been long esteemed in this country as the compilation of one of the greatest Arabic scholars of the time, the late Mr. Lane, the well-known translator of the 'Arabian Nights.' ... The present editor has enhanced the value of his relative's work by divesting the text of a great deal of extraneous matter introduced by way of comment, and prefixing an introduction."—*Times.*

"Mr. Poole is both a generous and a learned biographer.... Mr. Poole tells us the facts ... so far as it is possible for industry and criticism to ascertain them, and for literary skill to present them in a condensed and readable form."—*Englishman, Calcutta.*

Post 8vo, pp. vi.—368, cloth, price 14s.

## MODERN INDIA AND THE INDIANS,

BEING A SERIES OF IMPRESSIONS, NOTES, AND ESSAYS.
By MONIER WILLIAMS, D.C.L.,
Hon. LL.D. of the University of Calcutta, Hon. Member of the Bombay Asiatic Society, Boden Professor of Sanskrit in the University of Oxford.
Third Edition, revised and augmented by considerable Additions, with Illustrations and a Map.

"In this volume we have the thoughtful impressions of a thoughtful man on some of the most important questions connected with our Indian Empire.... An enlightened observant man, travelling among an enlightened observant people, Professor Monier Williams has brought before the public in a pleasant form more of the manners and customs of the Queen's Indian subjects than we ever remember to have seen in any one work. He not only deserves the thanks of every Englishman for this able contribution to the study of Modern India—a subject with which we should be specially familiar—but he deserves the thanks of every Indian, Parsee or Hindu, Buddhist and Moslem, for his clear exposition of their manners, their creeds, and their necessities."—*Times.*

Post 8vo, pp. xliv.—376, cloth, price 14s.

## METRICAL TRANSLATIONS FROM SANSKRIT WRITERS,

With an Introduction, many Prose Versions, and Parallel Passages from Classical Authors.

By J. MUIR, C.I.E., D.C.L., LL.D., Ph.D.

"... An agreeable introduction to Hindu poetry."—*Times.*

"... A volume which may be taken as a fair illustration alike of the religious and moral sentiments and of the legendary lore of the best Sanskrit writers."—*Edinburgh Daily Review.*

Second Edition, post 8vo, pp. xxvi.—244, cloth, price 10s. 6d.

# THE GULISTAN;

## OR, ROSE GARDEN OF SHEKH MUSHLIU'D-DIN SADI OF SHIRAZ.

Translated for the First Time into Prose and Verse, with an Introductory Preface, and a Life of the Author, from the Atish Kadah,

### BY EDWARD B. EASTWICK, C.B., M.A., F.R.S., M.R.A.S.

"It is a very fair rendering of the original."—*Times.*

"The new edition has long been desired, and will be welcomed by all who take any interest in Oriental poetry. The *Gulistan* is a typical Persian verse-book of the highest order. Mr. Eastwick's rhymed translation . . . has long established itself in a secure position as the best version of Sadi's finest work."—*Academy.*

"It is both faithfully and gracefully executed."—*Tablet.*

---

In Two Volumes, post 8vo, pp. viii.—408 and viii.—348, cloth, price 28s.

# MISCELLANEOUS ESSAYS RELATING TO INDIAN SUBJECTS.

### BY BRIAN HOUGHTON HODGSON, ESQ., F.R.S.,

Late of the Bengal Civil Service; Corresponding Member of the Institute; Chevalier of the Legion of Honour; late British Minister at the Court of Nepal, &c., &c.

### CONTENTS OF VOL. I.

SECTION I.—On the Kocch, Bódó, and Dhimál Tribes.—Part I. Vocabulary.—Part II. Grammar.—Part III. Their Origin, Location, Numbers, Creed, Customs, Character, and Condition, with a General Description of the Climate they dwell in.—Appendix.

SECTION II.—On Himalayan Ethnology.—I. Comparative Vocabulary of the Languages of the Broken Tribes of Népál.—II. Vocabulary of the Dialects of the Kiranti Language.—III. Grammatical Analysis of the Váyu Language. The Váyu Grammar.—IV. Analysis of the Báhing Dialect of the Kiranti Language. The Báhing Grammar.—V. On the Váyu or Háyu Tribe of the Central Himaláya.—VI. On the Kiranti Tribe of the Central Himaláya.

### CONTENTS OF VOL. II.

SECTION III.—On the Aborigines of North-Eastern India. Comparative Vocabulary of the Tibetan, Bódó, and Gáró Tongues.

SECTION IV.—Aborigines of the North-Eastern Frontier.

SECTION V.—Aborigines of the Eastern Frontier.

SECTION VI.—The Indo-Chinese Borderers, and their connection with the Himalayans and Tibetans. Comparative Vocabulary of Indo-Chinese Borderers in Arakan. Comparative Vocabulary of Indo-Chinese Borderers in Tenasserim.

SECTION VII.—The Mongolian Affinities of the Caucasians.—Comparison and Analysis of Caucasian and Mongolian Words.

SECTION VIII.—Physical Type of Tibetans.

SECTION IX.—The Aborigines of Central India.—Comparative Vocabulary of the Aboriginal Languages of Central India.—Aborigines of the Eastern Ghats.—Vocabulary of some of the Dialects of the Hill and Wandering Tribes in the Northern Sircars.—Aborigines of the Nilgiris, with Remarks on their Affinities.—Supplement to the Nilgirian Vocabularies.—The Aborigines of Southern India and Ceylon.

SECTION X.—Route of Nepalese Mission to Pekin, with Remarks on the Water-Shed and Plateau of Tibet.

SECTION XI.—Route from Káthmándú, the Capital of Nepál, to Darjeeling in Sikim.—Memorandum relative to the Seven Cosis of Nepál.

SECTION XII.—Some Accounts of the Systems of Law and Police as recognised in the State of Nepál.

SECTION XIII.—The Native Method of making the Paper denominated Hindustan, Népálese.

SECTION XIV.—Pre-eminence of the Vernaculars; or, the Anglicists Answered; Being Letters on the Education of the People of India.

"For the study of the less-known races of India Mr. Brian Hodgson's 'Miscellaneous Essays' will be found very valuable both to the philologist and the ethnologist."—*Times.*

Third Edition, Two Vols., post 8vo, pp. viii.—268 and viii.—326, cloth, price 21s.

## THE LIFE OR LEGEND OF GAUDAMA,

THE BUDDHA OF THE BURMESE. With Annotations.

The Ways to Neibban, and Notice on the Phongyies or Burmese Monks.

BY THE RIGHT REV. P. BIGANDET,

Bishop of Ramatha, Vicar-Apostolic of Ava and Pegu.

"The work is furnished with copious notes, which not only illustrate the subject-matter, but form a perfect encyclopædia of Buddhist lore."—*Times.*

"A work which will furnish European students of Buddhism with a most valuable help in the prosecution of their investigations."—*Edinburgh Daily Review.*

"Bishop Bigandet's invaluable work."—*Indian Antiquary.*

"Viewed in this light, its importance is sufficient to place students of the subject under a deep obligation to its author."—*Calcutta Review.*

"This work is one of the greatest authorities upon Buddhism."—*Dublin Review.*

---

Post 8vo, pp. xxiv.—420, cloth, price 18s.

## CHINESE BUDDHISM.

A VOLUME OF SKETCHES, HISTORICAL AND CRITICAL.

BY J. EDKINS, D.D.

Author of "China's Place in Philology," "Religion in China," &c., &c.

"It contains a vast deal of important information on the subject, such as is only to be gained by long-continued study on the spot."—*Athenæum.*

"Upon the whole, we know of no work comparable to it for the extent of its original research, and the simplicity with which this complicated system of philosophy, religion, literature, and ritual is set forth."—*British Quarterly Review.*

"The whole volume is replete with learning. . . . It deserves most careful study from all interested in the history of the religions of the world, and expressly of those who are concerned in the propagation of Christianity. Dr. Edkins notices in terms of just condemnation the exaggerated praise bestowed upon Buddhism by recent English writers."—*Record.*

---

Post 8vo, pp. 496, cloth, price 18s.

## LINGUISTIC AND ORIENTAL ESSAYS.

WRITTEN FROM THE YEAR 1846 TO 1878.

BY ROBERT NEEDHAM CUST,

Late Member of Her Majesty's Indian Civil Service; Hon. Secretary to the Royal Asiatic Society;
and Author of "The Modern Languages of the East Indies."

"We know none who has described Indian life, especially the life of the natives, with so much learning, sympathy, and literary talent."—*Academy.*

"They seem to us to be full of suggestive and original remarks."—*St. James's Gazette.*

"His book contains a vast amount of information. The result of thirty-five years of inquiry, reflection, and speculation, and that on subjects as full of fascination as of food for thought."—*Tablet.*

"Exhibit such a thorough acquaintance with the history and antiquities of India as to entitle him to speak as one having authority."—*Edinburgh Daily Review.*

"The author speaks with the authority of personal experience. . . . It is this constant association with the country and the people which gives such a vividness to many of the pages."—*Athenæum.*

Post 8vo, pp. civ.—348, cloth, price 18s.
## BUDDHIST BIRTH STORIES; or, Jataka Tales.
The Oldest Collection of Folk-lore Extant:
BEING THE JATAKATTHAVANNANA,
For the first time Edited in the original Pāli.
BY V. FAUSBOLL;
And Translated by T. W. RHYS DAVIDS.
Translation. Volume I.

"These are tales supposed to have been told by the Buddha of what he had seen and heard in his previous births. They are probably the nearest representatives of the original Aryan stories from which sprang the folk-lore of Europe as well as India. The introduction contains a most interesting disquisition on the migrations of these fables, tracing their reappearance in the various groups of folk-lore legends. Among other old friends, we meet with a version of the Judgment of Solomon."—*Times.*

"It is now some years since Mr. Rhys Davids asserted his right to be heard on this subject by his able article on Buddhism in the new edition of the 'Encyclopædia Britannica.'"—*Leeds Mercury.*

"All who are interested in Buddhist literature ought to feel deeply indebted to Mr. Rhys Davids. His well-established reputation as a Pali scholar is a sufficient guarantee for the fidelity of his version, and the style of his translations is deserving of high praise."—*Academy.*

"No more competent expositor of Buddhism could be found than Mr. Rhys Davids. In the Jātaka book we have, then, a priceless record of the earliest imaginative literature of our race; and . . . it presents to us a nearly complete picture of the social life and customs and popular beliefs of the common people of Aryan tribes, closely related to ourselves, just as they were passing through the first stages of civilisation."—*St. James's Gazette.*

Post 8vo, pp. xxviii.—362, cloth, price 14s.
## A TALMUDIC MISCELLANY;
OR, A THOUSAND AND ONE EXTRACTS FROM THE TALMUD, THE MIDRASHIM, AND THE KABBALAH.
Compiled and Translated by PAUL ISAAC HERSHON,
Author of "Genesis According to the Talmud," &c.
With Notes and Copious Indexes.

"To obtain in so concise and handy a form as this volume a general idea of the Talmud is a boon to Christians at least."—*Times.*

"Its peculiar and popular character will make it attractive to general readers. Mr. Hershon is a very competent scholar. . . . Contains samples of the good, bad, and indifferent, and especially extracts that throw light upon the Scriptures."—*British Quarterly Review.*

"Will convey to English readers a more complete and truthful notion of the Talmud than any other work that has yet appeared."—*Daily News.*

"Without overlooking in the slightest the several attractions of the previous volumes of the 'Oriental Series,' we have no hesitation in saying that this surpasses them all in interest."—*Edinburgh Daily Review.*

"Mr. Hershon has . . . thus given English readers what is, we believe, a fair set of specimens which they can test for themselves."—*The Record.*

"This book is by far the best fitted in the present state of knowledge to enable the general reader to gain a fair and unbiassed conception of the multifarious contents of the wonderful miscellany which can only be truly understood—so Jewish pride asserts—by the life-long devotion of scholars of the Chosen People."—*Inquirer.*

"The value and importance of this volume consist in the fact that scarcely a single extract is given in its pages but throws some light, direct or refracted, upon those Scriptures which are the common heritage of Jew and Christian alike."—*John Bull.*

"It is a capital specimen of Hebrew scholarship; a monument of learned, loving, light-giving labour."—*Jewish Herald.*

Post 8vo, pp. xii.—228, cloth, price 7s. 6d.

## THE CLASSICAL POETRY OF THE JAPANESE.
### By BASIL HALL CHAMBERLAIN,
Author of "Yeigo Heñkaku Shirañ."

"A very curious volume. The author has manifestly devoted much labour to the task of studying the poetical literature of the Japanese, and rendering characteristic specimens into English verse."—*Daily News.*

"Mr. Chamberlain's volume is, so far as we are aware, the first attempt which has been made to interpret the literature of the Japanese to the Western world. It is to the classical poetry of Old Japan that we must turn for indigenous Japanese thought, and in the volume before us we have a selection from that poetry rendered into graceful English verse."—*Tablet.*

"It is undoubtedly one of the best translations of lyric literature which has appeared during the close of the last year."—*Celestial Empire.*

"Mr. Chamberlain set himself a difficult task when he undertook to reproduce Japanese poetry in an English form. But he has evidently laboured *con amore*, and his efforts are successful to a degree."—*London and China Express.*

---

Post 8vo, pp. xii.—164, cloth, price 10s. 6d.

## THE HISTORY OF ESARHADDON (Son of Sennacherib),
### KING OF ASSYRIA, B.C. 681–668.

Translated from the Cuneiform Inscriptions upon Cylinders and Tablets in the British Museum Collection; together with a Grammatical Analysis of each Word, Explanations of the Ideographs by Extracts from the Bi-Lingual Syllabaries, and List of Eponyms, &c.

### By ERNEST A. BUDGE, B.A., M.R.A.S.,
Assyrian Exhibitioner, Christ's College, Cambridge.

"Students of scriptural archæology will also appreciate the 'History of Esarhaddon.'"—*Times.*

"There is much to attract the scholar in this volume. It does not pretend to popularise studies which are yet in their infancy. Its primary object is to translate, but it does not assume to be more than tentative, and it offers both to the professed Assyriologist and to the ordinary non-Assyriological Semitic scholar the means of controlling its results."—*Academy.*

"Mr. Budge's book is, of course, mainly addressed to Assyrian scholars and students. They are not, it is to be feared, a very numerous class. But the more thanks are due to him on that account for the way in which he has acquitted himself in his laborious task."—*Tablet.*

---

Post 8vo, pp. 448, cloth, price 21s.

## THE MESNEVI
(Usually known as THE MESNEVIYI SHERIF, or HOLY MESNEVI)
### OF
### MEVLANA (OUR LORD) JELALU 'D-DIN MUHAMMED ER-RUMI.
Book the First.

*Together with some Account of the Life and Acts of the Author, of his Ancestors, and of his Descendants.*

Illustrated by a Selection of Characteristic Anecdotes, as Collected by their Historian,

MEVLANA SHEMSU-'D-DIN AHMED, EL EFLAKI, EL 'ARIFI.

Translated, and the Poetry Versified, in English,
### By JAMES W. REDHOUSE, M.R.A.S., &c.

"A complete treasury of occult Oriental lore."—*Saturday Review.*

"This book will be a very valuable help to the reader ignorant of Persia, who is desirous of obtaining an insight into a very important department of the literature extant in that language."—*Tablet.*

Post 8vo, pp. xvi.—280, cloth, price 6s.

## EASTERN PROVERBS AND EMBLEMS
### ILLUSTRATING OLD TRUTHS.
By Rev. J. LONG,
Member of the Bengal Asiatic Society, F.R.G.S.

"We regard the book as valuable, and wish for it a wide circulation and attentive reading."—*Record*.
"Altogether, it is quite a feast of good things."—*Globe*.
"It is full of interesting matter."—*Antiquary*.

Post 8vo, pp. viii.—270, cloth, price 7s. 6d.

## INDIAN POETRY;

Containing a New Edition of the "Indian Song of Songs," from the Sanscrit of the "Gita Govinda" of Jayadeva; Two Books from "The Iliad of India" (Mahabharata), "Proverbial Wisdom" from the Shlokas of the Hitopadesa, and other Oriental Poems.

By EDWIN ARNOLD, C.S.I., Author of "The Light of Asia."

"In this new volume of Messrs. Trübner's Oriental Series, Mr. Edwin Arnold does good service by illustrating, through the medium of his musical English melodies, the power of Indian poetry to stir European emotions. The 'Indian Song of Songs' is not unknown to scholars. Mr. Arnold will have introduced it among popular English poems. Nothing could be more graceful and delicate than the shades by which Krishna is portrayed in the gradual process of being weaned by the love of

'Beautiful Radha, jasmine-bosomed Radha,'

from the allurements of the forest nymphs, in whom the five senses are typified."—*Times*.

"No other English poet has ever thrown his genius and his art so thoroughly into the work of translating Eastern ideas as Mr. Arnold has done in his splendid paraphrases of language contained in these mighty epics."—*Daily Telegraph*.

"The poem abounds with imagery of Eastern luxuriousness and sensuousness; the air seems laden with the spicy odours of the tropics, and the verse has a richness and a melody sufficient to captivate the senses of the dullest."—*Standard*.

"The translator, while producing a very enjoyable poem, has adhered with tolerable fidelity to the original text."—*Overland Mail*.

"We certainly wish Mr. Arnold success in his attempt 'to popularise Indian classics,' that being, as his preface tells us, the goal towards which he bends his efforts."—*Allen's Indian Mail*.

Post 8vo, pp. xvi.—296, cloth, price 10s. 6d.

## THE MIND OF MENCIUS;
### Or, POLITICAL ECONOMY FOUNDED UPON MORAL PHILOSOPHY.

A Systematic Digest of the Doctrines of the Chinese Philosopher Mencius.

Translated from the Original Text and Classified, with Comments and Explanations,

By the Rev. ERNST FABER, Rhenish Mission Society.

Translated from the German, with Additional Notes,

By the Rev. A. B. HUTCHINSON, C.M.S., Church Mission, Hong Kong.

"Mr. Faber is already well known in the field of Chinese studies by his digest of the doctrines of Confucius. The value of this work will be perceived when it is remembered that at no time since relations commenced between China and the West has the former been so powerful—we had almost said aggressive—as now. For those who will give it careful study, Mr. Faber's work is one of the most valuable of the excellent series to which it belongs."—*Nature*.

*TRÜBNER'S ORIENTAL SERIES.*

Post 8vo, pp. 336, cloth, price 16s.

# THE RELIGIONS OF INDIA.

### By A. BARTH.

Translated from the French with the authority and assistance of the Author.

The author has, at the request of the publishers, considerably enlarged the work for the translator, and has added the literature of the subject to date; the translation may, therefore, be looked upon as an equivalent of a new and improved edition of the original.

"Is not only a valuable manual of the religions of India, which marks a distinct step in the treatment of the subject, but also a useful work of reference."—*Academy.*

"This volume is a reproduction, with corrections and additions, of an article contributed by the learned author two years ago to the 'Encyclopédie des Sciences Religieuses.' It attracted much notice when it first appeared, and is generally admitted to present the best summary extant of the vast subject with which it deals."—*Tablet.*

"This is not only on the whole the best but the only manual of the religions of India, apart from Buddhism, which we have in English. The present work . . . shows not only great knowledge of the facts and power of clear exposition, but also great insight into the inner history and the deeper meaning of the great religion for it is in reality only one, which it proposes to describe."—*Modern Review.*

"The merit of the work has been emphatically recognised by the most authoritative Orientalists, both in this country and on the continent of Europe. But probably there are few Indianists (if we may use the word) who would not derive a good deal of information from it, and especially from the extensive bibliography provided in the notes."—*Dublin Review.*

"Such a sketch M. Barth has drawn with a master-hand."—*Critic (New York).*

---

Post 8vo, pp. viii.—152, cloth, price 6s.

# HINDU PHILOSOPHY.

### The SĀNKHYA KĀRIKA of IS'WARA KRISHNA.

An Exposition of the System of Kapila, with an Appendix on the Nyāya and Vais'eshika Systems.

### By JOHN DAVIES, M.A. (Cantab.), M.R.A.S.

The system of Kapila contains nearly all that India has produced in the department of pure philosophy.

"The non-Orientalist . . . finds in Mr. Davies a patient and learned guide who leads him into the intricacies of the philosophy of India, and supplies him with a clue that he may not be lost in them. In the preface he states that the system of Kapila is the 'earliest attempt on record to give an answer, from reason alone, to the mysterious questions which arise in every thoughtful mind about the origin of the world, the nature and relations of man and his future destiny,' and in his learned and able notes he exhibits 'the connection of the Sankhya system with the philosophy of Spinoza,' and 'the connection of the system of Kapila with that of Schopenhauer and Von Hartmann.'"—*Foreign Church Chronicle.*

"Mr. Davies's volume on Hindu Philosophy is an undoubted gain to all students of the development of thought. The system of Kapila, which is here given in a translation from the Sānkhya Kārikā, is the only contribution of India to pure philosophy. . . . Presents many points of deep interest to the student of comparative philosophy, and without Mr. Davies's lucid interpretation it would be difficult to appreciate these points in any adequate manner."—*Saturday Review.*

"We welcome Mr. Davies's book as a valuable addition to our philosophical library."—*Notes and Queries.*

Post 8vo, pp. x.—130, cloth, price 6s.

## A MANUAL OF HINDU PANTHEISM. VEDÂNTASÂRA.

Translated, with copious Annotations,

By MAJOR G. A. JACOB,

Bombay Staff Corps; Inspector of Army Schools.

The design of this little work is to provide for missionaries, and for others who, like them, have little leisure for original research, an accurate summary of the doctrines of the Vedânta.

"The modest title of Major Jacob's work conveys but an inadequate idea of the vast amount of research embodied in his notes to the text of the Vedântasara. So copious, indeed, are these, and so much collateral matter do they bring to bear on the subject, that the diligent student will rise from their perusal with a fairly adequate view of Hindû philosophy generally. His work ... is one of the best of its kind that we have seen."—*Calcutta Review.*

---

Post 8vo, pp. xii.—154, cloth, price 7s. 6d.

## TSUNI—||GOAM:

### THE SUPREME BEING OF THE KHOI-KHOI.

By THEOPHILUS HAHN, Ph.D.,

Custodian of the Grey Collection, Cape Town; Corresponding Member of the Geogr. Society, Dresden; Corresponding Member of the Anthropological Society, Vienna, &c., &c.

"The first instalment of Dr. Hahn's labours will be of interest, not at the Cape only, but in every University of Europe. It is, in fact, a most valuable contribution to the comparative study of religion and mythology. Accounts of their religion and mythology were scattered about in various books; these have been carefully collected by Dr. Hahn and printed in his second chapter, enriched and improved by what he has been able to collect himself."—*Prof. Max Müller in the Nineteenth Century.*

"It is full of good things."—*St. James's Gazette.*

---

In Four Volumes. Post 8vo, Vol. I., pp. xii.—392, cloth, price 12s. 6d., Vol. II., pp. vi.—408, cloth, price 12s. 6d., Vol. III., pp. viii.—414, cloth, price 12s. 6d., Vol. IV., pp. viii.—340, cloth, price 10s. 6d.

## A COMPREHENSIVE COMMENTARY TO THE QURAN.

### TO WHICH IS PREFIXED SALE'S PRELIMINARY DISCOURSE, WITH ADDITIONAL NOTES AND EMENDATIONS.

Together with a Complete Index to the Text, Preliminary Discourse, and Notes.

By Rev. E. M. WHERRY, M.A., Lodiana.

"As Mr. Wherry's book is intended for missionaries in India, it is no doubt well that they should be prepared to meet, if they can, the ordinary arguments and interpretations, and for this purpose Mr. Wherry's additions will prove useful."—*Saturday Review.*

*TRÜBNER'S ORIENTAL SERIES.*

---

Post 8vo, pp. vi.—208, cloth, price 8s. 6d.

## THE BHAGAVAD-GÎTÂ.

Translated, with Introduction and Notes.

By JOHN DAVIES, M.A. (Cantab.)

"Let us add that his translation of the Bhagavad Gîtâ is, as we judge, the best that has as yet appeared in English, and that his Philological Notes are of quite peculiar value."—*Dublin Review.*

---

Post 8vo, pp. 96, cloth, price 5s.

## THE QUATRAINS OF OMAR KHAYYAM.

Translated by E. H. WHINFIELD, M.A.,

Barrister-at-Law, late H.M. Bengal Civil Service.

---

Post 8vo, pp. xxxii.—336, cloth, price 10s. 6d.

## THE QUATRAINS OF OMAR KHAYYAM.

The Persian Text, with an English Verse Translation.

By E. H. WHINFIELD, late of the Bengal Civil Service.

"Mr. Whinfield has executed a difficult task with considerable success, and his version contains much that will be new to those who only know Mr. Fitzgerald's delightful selection."—*Academy.*

"The most prominent features in the Quatrains are their profound agnosticism, combined with a fatalism based more on philosophic than religious grounds, their Epicureanism and the spirit of universal tolerance and charity which animates them."—*Calcutta Review.*

---

Post 8vo, pp. xxiv.—268, cloth, price 9s.

## THE PHILOSOPHY OF THE UPANISHADS AND ANCIENT INDIAN METAPHYSICS.

As exhibited in a series of Articles contributed to the *Calcutta Review.*

By ARCHIBALD EDWARD GOUGH, M.A., Lincoln College, Oxford;
Principal of the Calcutta Madrasa.

"For practical purposes this is perhaps the most important of the works that have thus far appeared in 'Trübner's Oriental Series.' . . . We cannot doubt that for all who may take it up the work must be one of profound interest."—*Saturday Review.*

---

In Two Volumes. Vol. I., post 8vo, pp. xxiv.—230, cloth, price 7s. 6d.

## A COMPARATIVE HISTORY OF THE EGYPTIAN AND MESOPOTAMIAN RELIGIONS.

By Dr. C. P. TIELE.

Vol. I.—HISTORY OF THE EGYPTIAN RELIGION.

Translated from the Dutch with the Assistance of the Author.

By JAMES BALLINGAL.

"It places in the hands of the English readers a history of Egyptian Religion which is very complete, which is based on the best materials, and which has been illustrated by the latest results of research. In this volume there is a great deal of information, as well as independent investigation, for the trustworthiness of which Dr. Tiele's name is in itself a guarantee; and the description of the successive religions under the Old Kingdom, the Middle Kingdom, and the New Kingdom, is given in a manner which is scholarly and minute."—*Scotsman.*

Post 8vo, pp. xii.—302, cloth, price 8s. 6d.

## YUSUF AND ZULAIKHA.

A POEM BY JAMI.

Translated from the Persian into English Verse.

BY RALPH T. H. GRIFFITH.

"Mr. Griffith, who has done already good service as translator into verse from the Sanskrit, has done further good work in this translation from the Persian, and he has evidently shown not a little skill in his rendering the quaint and very oriental style of his author into our more prosaic, less figurative, language. . . . The work, besides its intrinsic merits, is of importance as being one of the most popular and famous poems of Persia, and that which is read in all the independent native schools of India where Persian is taught."—*Scotsman.*

---

Post 8vo, pp. viii.—266, cloth, price 9s.

## LINGUISTIC ESSAYS.

BY CARL ABEL.

"An entirely novel method of dealing with philosophical questions and impart real human interest to the otherwise dry technicalities of the science."—*Standard.*

"Dr. Abel is an opponent from whom it is pleasant to differ, for he writes with enthusiasm and temper, and his mastery over the English language fits him to be a champion of unpopular doctrines."—*Athenæum.*

---

Post 8vo, pp. ix.—281, cloth, price 10s. 6d.

## THE SARVA-DARSANA-SAMGRAHA;

OR, REVIEW OF THE DIFFERENT SYSTEMS OF HINDU PHILOSOPHY.

BY MADHAVA ACHARYA.

Translated by E. B. COWELL, M.A., Professor of Sanskrit in the University of Cambridge, and A. E. GOUGH, M.A., Professor of Philosophy in the Presidency College, Calcutta.

This work is an interesting specimen of Hindu critical ability. The author successively passes in review the sixteen philosophical systems current in the fourteenth century in the South of India; and he gives what appears to him to be their most important tenets.

"The translation is trustworthy throughout. A protracted sojourn in India, where there is a living tradition, has familiarised the translators with Indian thought."—*Athenæum.*

---

Post 8vo, pp. lxv.—368, cloth, price 14s.

## TIBETAN TALES DERIVED FROM INDIAN SOURCES.

Translated from the Tibetan of the KAH-GYUR.

BY F. ANTON VON SCHIEFNER.

Done into English from the German, with an Introduction,

BY W. R. S. RALSTON, M.A.

"Mr. Ralston, whose name is so familiar to all lovers of Russian folk-lore, has supplied some interesting Western analogies and parallels, drawn, for the most part, from Slavonic sources, to the Eastern folk-tales, culled from the Kahgyur, one of the divisions of the Tibetan sacred books."—*Academy.*

"The translation . . . could scarcely have fallen into better hands. An Introduction . . . gives the leading facts in the lives of those scholars who have given their attention to gaining a knowledge of the Tibetan literature and language."—*Calcutta Review.*

"Ought to interest all who care for the East, for amusing stories, or for comparative folk-lore."—*Pall Mall Gazette.*

Post 8vo, pp. xvi.—224, cloth, price 9s.

## UDÂNAVARGA.

A COLLECTION OF VERSES FROM THE BUDDHIST CANON.

Compiled by DHARMATRÂTA.

BEING THE NORTHERN BUDDHIST VERSION OF DHAMMAPADA.

Translated from the Tibetan of Bkah-hgyur, with Notes, and Extracts from the Commentary of Pradjnavarman,

By W. WOODVILLE ROCKHILL.

"Mr. Rockhill's present work is the first from which assistance will be gained for a more accurate understanding of the Pali text; it is, in fact, as yet the only term of comparison available to us. The 'Udânavarga,' the Thibetan version, was originally discovered by the late M. Schiefner, who published the Tibetan text, and had intended adding a translation, an intention frustrated by his death, but which has been carried out by Mr. Rockhill. . . . Mr. Rockhill may be congratulated for having well accomplished a difficult task."—*Saturday Review.*

---

In Two Volumes, post 8vo, pp. xxiv.—566, cloth, accompanied by a Language Map, price 25s.

## A SKETCH OF THE MODERN LANGUAGES OF AFRICA.

By ROBERT NEEDHAM CUST,

Barrister-at-Law, and late of Her Majesty's Indian Civil Service.

"Any one at all interested in African languages cannot do better than get Mr. Cust's book. It is encyclopædic in its scope, and the reader gets a start clear away in any particular language, and is left free to add to the initial sum of knowledge there collected."—*Natal Mercury.*

"Mr. Cust has contrived to produce a work of value to linguistic students."—*Nature.*

---

Third Edition. Post 8vo, pp. xv.-250, cloth, price 7s. 6d.

## OUTLINES OF THE HISTORY OF RELIGION TO THE SPREAD OF THE UNIVERSAL RELIGIONS.

By C. P. TIELE,

Doctor of Theology, Professor of the History of Religions in the University of Leyden.

Translated from the Dutch by J. ESTLIN CARPENTER, M.A.

"Few books of its size contain the result of so much wide thinking, able and laborious study, or enable the reader to gain a better bird's-eye view of the latest results of investigations into the religious history of nations. As Professor Tiele modestly says, 'In this little book are outlines—pencil sketches, I might say—nothing more.' But there are some men whose sketches from a thumb-nail are of far more worth than an enormous canvas covered with the crude painting of others, and it is easy to see that these pages, full of information, these sentences, cut and perhaps also dry, short and clear, condense the fruits of long and thorough research."—*Scotsman.*

Post 8vo, pp. xii.—312, with Maps and Plan, cloth, price 14s.
## A HISTORY OF BURMA.
Including Burma Proper, Pegu, Taungu, Tenasserim, and Arakan. From the Earliest Time to the End of the First War with British India.

By LIEUT.-GEN. SIR ARTHUR P. PHAYRE, G.C.M.G., K.C.S.I., and C.B.,
Membre Correspondant de la Société Académique Indo-Chinoise de France.

"Sir Arthur Phayre's contribution to Trübner's Oriental Series supplies a recognised want, and its appearance has been looked forward to for many years. . . . General Phayre deserves great credit for the patience and industry which has resulted in this History of Burma."—*Saturday Review.*

---

Third Edition. Post 8vo, pp. 276, cloth, price 7s. 6d.
## RELIGION IN CHINA.
### By JOSEPH EDKINS, D.D., PEKING.

Containing a Brief Account of the Three Religions of the Chinese, with Observations on the Prospects of Christian Conversion amongst that People.

"Dr. Edkins has been most careful in noting the varied and often complex phases of opinion, so as to give an account of considerable value of the subject."—*Scotsman.*

"As a missionary, it has been part of Dr. Edkins' duty to study the existing religions in China, and his long residence in the country has enabled him to acquire an intimate knowledge of them as they at present exist."—*Saturday Review.*

"Dr. Edkins' valuable work, of which this is a second and revised edition, has, from the time that it was published, been the standard authority upon the subject of which it treats."—*Nonconformist.*

"Dr. Edkins . . . may now be fairly regarded as among the first authorities on Chinese religion and language."—*British Quarterly Review.*

---

Post 8vo, pp. x.-274, cloth, price 9s.
## THE LIFE OF THE BUDDHA AND THE EARLY HISTORY OF HIS ORDER.
Derived from Tibetan Works in the Bkah-hgyur and Bstan-hgyur. Followed by notices on the Early History of Tibet and Khoten.

Translated by W. W. ROCKHILL, Second Secretary U.S. Legation in China.

"The volume bears testimony to the diligence and fulness with which the author has consulted and tested the ancient documents bearing upon his remarkable subject."—*Times.*

"Will be appreciated by those who devote themselves to those Buddhist studies which have of late years taken in these Western regions so remarkable a development. Its matter possesses a special interest as being derived from ancient Tibetan works, some portions of which, here analysed and translated, have not yet attracted the attention of scholars. The volume is rich in ancient stories bearing upon the world's renovation and the origin of castes, as recorded in these venerable authorities."—*Daily News.*

---

Third Edition. Post 8vo, pp. viii.-464, cloth, price 16s.
## THE SANKHYA APHORISMS OF KAPILA,
With Illustrative Extracts from the Commentaries.

Translated by J. R. BALLANTYNE, LL.D., late Principal of the Benares College.

### Edited by FITZEDWARD HALL.

"The work displays a vast expenditure of labour and scholarship, for which students of Hindoo philosophy have every reason to be grateful to Dr. Hall and the publishers."—*Calcutta Review.*

In Two Volumes, post 8vo, pp. cviii.-242, and viii.-370, cloth, price 24s.
Dedicated by permission to H.R.H. the Prince of Wales.

## BUDDHIST RECORDS OF THE WESTERN WORLD,

Translated from the Chinese of Hiuen Tsiang (A.D. 629).

### By SAMUEL BEAL, B.A.,

(Trin. Coll., Camb.); R.N. (Retired Chaplain and N.I.); Professor of Chinese, University College, London; Rector of Wark, Northumberland, &c.

An eminent Indian authority writes respecting this work:—"Nothing more can be done in elucidating the History of India until Mr. Beal's translation of the 'Si-yu-ki' appears."

"It is a strange freak of historical preservation that the best account of the condition of India at that ancient period has come down to us in the books of travel written by the Chinese pilgrims, of whom Hwen Thsang is the best known."—*Times*.

---

Post 8vo, pp. xlviii.-398, cloth, price 12s.

## THE ORDINANCES OF MANU.

Translated from the Sanskrit, with an Introduction.

### By the late A. C. BURNELL, Ph.D., C.I.E.

Completed and Edited by E. W. HOPKINS, Ph.D., of Columbia College, N.Y.

"This work is full of interest; while for the student of sociology and the science of religion it is full of importance. It is a great boon to get so notable a work in so accessible a form, admirably edited, and competently translated."—*Scotsman*.

"Few men were more competent than Burnell to give us a really good translation of this well-known law book, first rendered into English by Sir William Jones. Burnell was not only an independent Sanskrit scholar, but an experienced lawyer, and he joined to these two important qualifications the rare faculty of being able to express his thoughts in clear and trenchant English. . . . We ought to feel very grateful to Dr. Hopkins for having given us all that could be published of the translation left by Burnell."—F. MAX MÜLLER in the *Academy*.

---

Post 8vo, pp. xii.-234, cloth, price 9s.

## THE LIFE AND WORKS OF ALEXANDER CSOMA DE KOROS,

Between 1819 and 1842. With a Short Notice of all his Published and Unpublished Works and Essays. From Original and for most part Unpublished Documents.

### By THEODORE DUKA, M.D., F.R.C.S. (Eng.), Surgeon-Major H.M.'s Bengal Medical Service, Retired, &c.

"Not too soon have Messrs. Trübner added to their valuable Oriental Series a history of the life and works of one of the most gifted and devoted of Oriental students, Alexander Csoma de Koros. It is forty-three years since his death, and though an account of his career was demanded soon after his decease, it has only now appeared in the important memoir of his compatriot, Dr. Duka."—*Bookseller*.

In Two Volumes, post 8vo, pp. xii.-318 and vi.-312, cloth, price 21s.

# MISCELLANEOUS PAPERS RELATING TO INDO-CHINA.

Reprinted from "Dalrymple's Oriental Repertory," "Asiatic Researches," and the "Journal of the Asiatic Society of Bengal."

*CONTENTS OF VOL. I.*

I.—Some Accounts of Quedah. By Michael Topping.
II.—Report made to the Chief and Council of Balambangan, by Lieut. James Barton, of his several Surveys.
III.—Substance of a Letter to the Court of Directors from Mr. John Jesse, dated July 20, 1775, at Borneo Proper.
IV.—Formation of the Establishment of Poolo Peenang.
V.—The Gold of Limong. By John Macdonald.
VI.—On Three Natural Productions of Sumatra. By John Macdonald.
VII.—On the Traces of the Hindu Language and Literature extant amongst the Malays. By William Marsden.
VIII.—Some Account of the Elastic Gum Vine of Prince-Wales Island. By James Howison.
IX.—A Botanical Description of Urceola Elastica, or Caoutchouc Vine of Sumatra and Pulo-Pinang. By William Roxburgh, M.D.
X.—An Account of the Inhabitants of the Poggy, or Nassau Islands, lying off Sumatra. By John Crisp.
XI.—Remarks on the Species of Pepper which are found on Prince-Wales Island. By William Hunter, M.D.
XII.—On the Languages and Literature of the Indo-Chinese Nations. By J. Leyden, M.D.
XIII.—Some Account of an Orang-Outang of remarkable height found on the Island of Sumatra. By Clarke Abel, M.D.
XIV.—Observations on the Geological Appearances and General Features of Portions of the Malayan Peninsula. By Captain James Low.
XV.—Short Sketch of the Geology of Pulo-Pinang and the Neighbouring Islands. By T. Ware.
XVI.—Climate of Singapore.
XVII.—Inscription on the Jetty at Singapore.
XVIII.—Extract of a Letter from Colonel J. Low.
XIX.—Inscription at Singapore.
XX.—An Account of Several Inscriptions found in Province Wellesley. By Lieut.-Col. James Low.
XXI.—Note on the Inscriptions from Singapore and Province Wellesley. By J. W. Laidlay.
XXII.—On an Inscription from Keddah. By Lieut.-Col. Low.
XXIII.—A Notice of the Alphabets of the Philippine Islands.
XXIV.—Succinct Review of the Observations of the Tides in the Indian Archipelago.
XXV.—Report on the Tin of the Province of Mergui. By Capt. G. B Tremenheere.
XXVI.—Report on the Manganese of Mergui Province. By Capt. G. B. Tremenheere.
XXVII.—Paragraphs to be added to Capt. G. B. Tremenheere's Report.
XXVIII.—Second Report on the Tin of Mergui. By Capt. G. B. Tremenheere.
XXIX.—Analysis of Iron Ores from Tavoy and Mergui, and of Limestone from Mergui. By Dr. A. Ure.
XXX.—Report of a Visit to the Pakchan River, and of some Tin Localities in the Southern Portion of the Tenasserim Provinces. By Capt. G. B. Tremenheere.
XXXI.—Report on a Route from the Mouth of the Pakchan to Krau, and thence across the Isthmus of Krau to the Gulf of Siam. By Capt. Al. Fraser and Capt. J. G. Forlong.
XXXII.—Report, &c., from Capt. G. B. Tremenheere on the Price of Mergui Tin Ore.
XXXIII.—Remarks on the Different Species of Orang-utan. By E. Blyth.
XXXIV.—Further Remarks. By E. Blyth.

## MISCELLANEOUS PAPERS RELATING TO INDO-CHINA—
### continued.

*CONTENTS OF VOL. II.*

XXXV.—Catalogue of Mammalia inhabiting the Malayan Peninsula and Islands. By Theodore Cantor, M.D.
XXXVI.—On the Local and Relative Geology of Singapore. By J. R. Logan.
XXXVII.—Catalogue of Reptiles inhabiting the Malayan Peninsula and Islands. By Theodore Cantor, M.D.
XXXVIII.—Some Account of the Botanical Collection brought from the Eastward, in 1841, by Dr. Cantor. By the late W. Griffith.
XXXIX.—On the Flat-Horned Taurine Cattle of S.E. Asia. By E. Blyth.
XL.—Note, by Major-General G. B. Tremenheere.
General Index.
Index of Vernacular Terms.
Index of Zoological Genera and Sub-Genera occurring in Vol. II.

"The papers treat of almost every aspect of Indo-China—its philology, economy, geography, geology—and constitute a very material and important contribution to our accessible information regarding that country and its people."—*Contemporary Review.*

---

Post 8vo, pp. xii.-72, cloth, price 5s.

## THE SATAKAS OF BHARTRIHARI.

Translated from the Sanskrit

By the REV. B. HALE WORTHAM, M.R.A.S.,

Rector of Eggesford, North Devon.

"A very interesting addition to Trübner's Oriental Series."—*Saturday Review.*
"Many of the Maxims in the book have a Biblical ring and beauty of expression."—*St. James' Gazette.*

---

Post 8vo, pp. xii.-180, cloth, price 6s.

## ANCIENT PROVERBS AND MAXIMS FROM BURMESE SOURCES;
### OR, THE NITI LITERATURE OF BURMA.

BY JAMES GRAY,

Author of "Elements of Pali Grammar," "Translation of the Dhammapada," &c.

The Sanscrit-Pâli word Nîti is equivalent to "conduct" in its abstract, and "guide" in its concrete signification. As applied to books, it is a general term for a treatise which includes maxims, pithy sayings, and didactic stories, intended as a guide to such matters of every-day life as form the character of an individual and influence him in his relations to his fellow-men. Treatises of this kind have been popular in all ages, and have served as a most effective medium of instruction.

*TRÜBNER'S ORIENTAL SERIES.*

---

Post 8vo, pp. xxxii. and 330, cloth, price 7s. 6d.

## MASNAVI I MA' NAVI:

THE SPIRITUAL COUPLETS OF MAULANA JALALU-'D-DIN MUHAMMAD I RUMI.

Translated and Abridged by E. H. WHINFIELD, M.A.,
Late of H.M. Bengal Civil Service.

---

Post 8vo, pp. viii. and 346, cloth, price 10s. 6d.

## MANAVA-DHARMA-CASTRA:
## THE CODE OF MANU.

ORIGINAL SANSKRIT TEXT, WITH CRITICAL NOTES.

BY J. JOLLY, Ph.D.,

Professor of Sanskrit in the University of Wurzburg; late Tagore Professor of Law in the University of Calcutta.

The date assigned by Sir William Jones to this Code—the well-known Great Law Book of the Hindus—is 1250–500 B.C., although the rules and precepts contained in it had probably existed as tradition for countless ages before. There has been no reliable edition of the Text for Students for many years past, and it is believed, therefore, that Prof. Jolly's work will supply a want long felt.

---

Post 8vo, pp. 215, cloth, price 7s. 6d.

## LEAVES FROM MY CHINESE SCRAP-BOOK.

BY FREDERIC HENRY BALFOUR.

Author of "Waifs and Strays from the Far East," "Taoist Texts," "Idiomatic Phrases in the Peking Colloquial," &c. &c.

---

*THE FOLLOWING WORKS ARE IN PREPARATION:—*

In Two Vols., post 8vo.

## ALBERUNI'S INDIA:

AN ACCOUNT OF ITS RELIGION, PHILOSOPHY, LITERATURE, GEOGRAPHY, CHRONOLOGY, ASTRONOMY, CUSTOMS, LAW, AND ASTROLOGY (ABOUT A.D. 1031).

TRANSLATED INTO ENGLISH.

With Notes and Indices by Prof. EDWARD SACHAU,
University of Berlin.

\*\*\* The Arabic Original, with an Index of the Sanskrit Words, Edited by Professor SACHAU, is in the press.

*TRÜBNER'S ORIENTAL SERIES.*

In Two Volumes, post 8vo.
## MISCELLANEOUS PAPERS RELATING TO INDO-CHINA.

Edited by R. ROST, Ph.D., &c. &c.,
Librarian to the India Office.

SECOND SERIES.

Reprinted for the Straits Branch of the Royal Asiatic Society from the Malayan "Miscellanies," the "Transactions and Journal" of the Batavian Society," and the "Journals" of the Asiatic Society of Bengal, and the Royal Geographical and Royal Asiatic Societies.

---

Post 8vo.
## THE LIFE OF HIUEN TSIANG.

BY THE SHAMANS HWUI LI AND YEN-TSUNG.

With a Preface containing an account of the Works of I-TSING.

BY SAMUEL BEAL, B.A.

(Trin. Coll., Camb.); Professor of Chinese, University College, London; Rector of Wark, Northumberland, &c.

Author of "Buddhist Records of the Western World," "The Romantic Legend of Sakya Budda," &c.

When the Pilgrim Hiuen Tsiang returned from his travels in India, he took up his abode in the Temple of "Great Benevolence;" this convent had been constructed by the Emperor in honour of the Empress, Wen-te-hau. After Hiuen Tsiang's death, his disciple, Hwui Li, composed a work which gave an account of his illustrious Master's travels; this work when he completed he buried, and refused to discover its place of concealment. But previous to his death he revealed its whereabouts to Yen-tsung, by whom it was finally revised and published. This is "The Life of Hiuen Tsiang." It is a valuable sequel to the Si-yu-ki, correcting and illustrating it in many particulars.

---

Post 8vo.
## A SKETCH OF THE MODERN LANGUAGES OF OCEANIA.

BY R. N. CUST, LL.D.

Author of "Modern Languages of the East," "Modern Languages of Africa," &c.

---

Post 8vo.
## ESSAYS ON THE INTERCOURSE OF THE CHINESE WITH WESTERN COUNTRIES IN THE MIDDLE AGES AND ON KINDRED SUBJECTS.

BY E. BRETSCHNEIDER, M.D.,
Formerly Physician of the Russian Legation at Pekin.

---

LONDON: TRÜBNER & CO., 57 AND 59 LUDGATE HILL.

# TRÜBNER'S
## ORIENTAL SERIES.

### V.

**Ballantyne Press**
BALLANTYNE, HANSON AND CO
EDINBURGH AND LONDON

# THE BIRTH OF THE WAR-GOD.

*A POEM BY KÁLIDÁSA.*

Translated from the Sanskrit into English Verse

BY

RALPH T. H. GRIFFITH, M.A.

PRINCIPAL OF BENARES COLLEGE.

Second Edition.

LONDON:
TRÜBNER & CO., LUDGATE HILL.
1879.
[*All rights reserved.*]

$$\frac{4591}{1879\,100}$$

# PREFACE.

OF the history of KÁLIDÁSA, to whom by general assent the KUMÁRA SAMBHAVA, or BIRTH OF THE WAR-GOD, is attributed, we know but little with any certainty; we can only gather from a memorial-verse which enumerates their names, that he was one of the 'Nine Precious Stones' that shone at the Court of VIKRAMÁDITYA, King of OUJEIN, in the half century immediately preceding the Christian era.* As the examination of arguments for and against the correctness of this date is not likely to interest general readers, I must request them to rest satisfied with the belief that about the time when VIRGIL and HORACE were shedding an undying lustre upon the reign of AUGUSTUS, our poet KÁLIDÁSA lived, loved, and sang, giving and taking honour, at the polished court of the no less munificent patron of Sanskrit literature, at the period of its highest perfection.

* [This date is much too early. It has been shown by H. Jacobi from the astrological data contained in the poem that the date of its composition cannot be placed earlier than about the middle of the fourth century A.D.]

Little as we know of Indian poetry, here and there an English reader may be found, who is not entirely unacquainted with the name or works of the author of the beautiful dramas of SAKONTALÁ and THE HERO AND THE NYMPH, the former of which has long enjoyed an European celebrity in the translation of SIR WILLIAM JONES, and the latter is one of the most charming of PROFESSOR WILSON's specimens of the Hindú Theatre; here and there even in England may be found a lover of the graceful, tender, picturesque, and fanciful, who knows something, and would gladly know more, of the sweet poet of the CLOUD MESSENGER, and THE SEASONS; whilst in Germany he has been deeply studied in the original, and enthusiastically admired in translation,— not the Orientalist merely, but the poet, the critic, the natural philosopher,—a GOETHE, a SCHLEGEL, a HUMBOLDT, having agreed, on account of his tenderness of feeling and his rich creative imagination, to set KÁLIDÁSA very high among the glorious company of the Sons of Song.*

That the poem which is now for the first time offered

---

\* Goethe says :

Willst du die Blüthe des frühen, die Früchte des späteren Jahres,
   Willst du was reizt und entzückt, willst du was sättigt und nährt,
Willst du den Himmel, die Erde, mit einem Namen begreifen;
   Nenn' ich Sakontalá, Dich, und so ist Alles gesagt.

See also Schlegel's Dramatic Literature, Lect. II., and Humboldt's Kosmos, Vol. II. p. 40, and note.

to the general reader, in an English dress, will not diminish this reputation is the translator's earnest hope, yet my admiration of the grace and beauty that pervade so much of the work must not allow me to deny that occasionally, even in the noble Sanskrit, if we judge him by an European standard, KÁLIDÁSA is bald and prosaic. Nor is this a defence of the translator at the expense of the poet. Fully am I conscious how far I am from being able adequately to reproduce the fanciful creation of the sweet singer of OUJEIN; that numerous beauties of thought and expression I may have passed by, mistaken, marred; that in many of the more elaborate descriptions my own versification is 'harsh as the jarring of a tuneless chord' compared with the melody of KÁLIDÁSA's rhythm, to rival whose sweetness and purity of language, so admirably adapted to the soft repose and celestial rosy hue of his pictures, would have tried all the fertility of resource, the artistic skill, and the exquisite ear of the author of LALLA ROOKH himself. I do not think this poem deserves, and I am sure it will not obtain, that admiration which the author's masterpieces already made known at once commanded; at all events, if the work itself is not inferior, it has not enjoyed the good fortune of having a JONES or a WILSON for translator.

It may be as well to inform the reader, before he wonder at the misnomer, that the BIRTH OF THE WAR-

GOD was either left unfinished by its author, or time has robbed us of the conclusion; the latter is the more probable supposition, tradition informing us that the poem originally consisted of twenty-two cantos, of which only seven now remain.*

I have derived great assistance in the work of translation from the Calcutta printed edition of the poem in the Library of the East-India House; but although the Sanskrit commentaries accompanying the text are sometimes of the greatest use in unravelling the author's meaning, they can scarcely claim infallibility; and, not unfrequently, are so matter-of-fact and prosaic, that I have not scrupled to think, or rather to feel, for myself. It is, however, PROFESSOR STENZLER's edition,† published under the auspices of the Oriental Translation Fund (a society that has liberally encouraged my own undertaking), that I have chiefly used. Valuable as this work is (and I will not disown my great obligations to it), it is much to be regretted that the extracts from the native commentators are so scanty, and the annotations so few and brief.

And now one word as to the manner in which I have endeavoured to perform my task. Though there is much,

[* Ten more cantos, of very inferior merit, have been published since this was written.]
† [With a Latin translation.]

I think, that might be struck out, to the advantage of the poem, this I have in no instance ventured to do, my aim having been to give the English reader as faithful a cast of the original as my own power and the nature of things would permit, and, without attempting to give word for word or line for line, to produce upon the imagination impressions similar to those which one who studies the work in Sanskrit would experience.

I will not seek to anticipate the critics, nor to deprecate their animadversions, by pointing out the beauties of the poet, or particularising the defects of him and his translator. That the former will be appreciated, and the latter kindly dealt with, late experience makes me confident; so that now, in the words of the Manager in the Prelude to the HERO AND THE NYMPH, " I have only to request the audience that they will listen to this work of KÁLIDÁSA with attention and kindness, in consideration of its subject and respect for the Author."

ADDERLEY LIBRARY, MARLBOROUGH COLLEGE,
*April*, 1853.

# PRELIMINARY NOTE.

## PRONUNCIATION.

As a general rule, the Sanskrit vowels are to be sounded like those of the Italian alphabet, except the short or unaccented *a*, which has the sound of that letter in the word *America:* "*pandit*," a learned man, being pronounced *pundit*.

*á*, long or accented ... like *a* in *father*.
*e* ........................ like *e* in *they*.
*i*, short or unaccented, like *i* in *pick*.
*í*, long or accented ... like *i* in *pique*.
*o* ........................ like *o* in *go*.
*u*, short or unaccented, like *u* in *full*.
*ú*, long or accented ... like *u* in *rule*.

The diphthongs *ai* and *au* are pronounced severally like *i* in *rise* and *ou* in *our*.

The consonants are sounded as in English. In the aspirates, however, the sound of *h* is kept distinct; *dh, th, ph, bh,* &c., being pronounced as in *red-hot, pent-house, up-hill, abhor,* &c. *G* is always hard, whatever vowel follows.

In HIMÁLAYA the accent is on the *second* syllable.

# THE BIRTH OF THE WAR-GOD.

## Canto First.

### UMÁ'S NATIVITY.

FAR in the north HIMÁLAYA, lifting high
His towery summits till they cleave the sky,
Spans the wide land from east to western sea,
Lord of the hills, instinct with deity.
For him, when PRITHU ruled in days of old
The rich earth, teeming with her gems and gold,
The vassal hills and MERU drained her breast,
To deck HIMÁLAYA, for they loved him best;
And earth, the mother, gave her store to fill
With herbs and sparkling ores the royal hill.

 Proud mountain-king! his diadem of snow
Dims not the beauty of his gems below.
For who can gaze upon the moon, and dare
To mark one spot less brightly glorious there?

Who, 'mid a thousand virtues, dares to blame
One shade of weakness in a hero's fame?
Oft, when the gleamings of his mountain brass
Flash through the clouds and tint them as they pass,
Those glories mock the hues of closing day,
And heaven's bright wantons hail their hour of play;
Try, ere the time, the magic of their glance,
And deck their beauty for the twilight dance.
Dear to the sylphs are the cool shadows thrown
By dark clouds wandering round the mountain's zone,
Till frightened by the storm and rain they seek
Eternal sunshine on each loftier peak.

   Far spread the wilds where eager hunters roam,
Tracking the lion to his dreary home.
For though the melting snow has washed away
The crimson blood-drops of the wounded prey,
Still the fair pearls that graced his forehead tell
Where the strong elephant, o'ermastered, fell,
And clinging to the lion's claws, betray,
Falling at every step, the mighty conqueror's way.
There birch-trees wave, that lend their friendly aid
To tell the passion of the love-lorn maid,
So quick to learn in metal tints to mark
Her hopes and fears upon the tender bark.

   List! breathing from each cave, HIMÁLAYA leads
The glorious hymn with all his whispering reeds,

Till heavenly minstrels raise their voice in song,
And swell his music as it floats along.
There the fierce elephant wounds the scented bough
To ease the torment of his burning brow;
And bleeding pines their odorous gum distil
To breathe rare fragrance o'er the sacred hill.

   There magic herbs pour forth their streaming light
From mossy caverns through the darksome night,
And lend a torch to guide the trembling maid
Where waits her lover in the leafy shade.
Yet hath he caves within whose inmost cells
In tranquil rest the murky darkness dwells,
And, like the night-bird, spreads the brooding wing
Safe in the shelter of the mountain-king,
Unscorned, uninjured; for the good and great
Spurn not the suppliant for his lowly state.

   Why lingers yet the heavenly minstrel's bride
On the wild path that skirts HIMÁLAYA's side?
Cold to her tender feet—oh, cold—the snow,
Why should her steps — her homeward steps — be slow?
'Tis that her slender ankles scarce can bear
The weight of beauty that impedes her there;
Each rounded limb, and all her peerless charms,
That broad full bosom, those voluptuous arms.

E'en the wild kine that roam his forests bring
The royal symbols to the mountain-king.
With tails outspread, their bushy streaming hair
Flashes like moonlight through the parted air.
What monarch's fan more glorious might there be,
More meet to grace a king as proud as he?

There, when the nymphs, within the cave's recess,
In modest fear their gentle limbs undress,
Thick clouds descending yield a friendly screen,
And blushing beauty bares her breast unseen.

With pearly dewdrops GANGÁ loads the gale
That waves the dark pines towering o'er the vale,
And breathes in welcome freshness o'er the face
Of wearied hunters when they quit the chase.

So far aloft, amid Himálayan steeps,
Couched on the tranquil pool the lotus sleeps,
That the bright SEVEN who star the northern sky
Cull the fair blossoms from their seats on high;
And when the sun pours forth his morning glow
In streams of glory from his path below,
They gain new beauty as his kisses break
His darlings' slumber on the mountain lake.

Well might that ancient hill by merit claim
The power and glory of a monarch's name;

## UMÁ'S NATIVITY.

Nurse of pure herbs that grace each holy rite,
Earth's meetest bearer of unyielding might.
The Lord of Life for this ordained him king,
And bade him share the sacred offering.

Gladly obedient to the law divine,
He chose a consort to prolong his line.
No child of earth, born of the Sages' will,
The fair nymph MENÁ pleased the sovran hill.
To her he sued, nor was his prayer denied,
The Saints' beloved was the mountain's bride.
Crowned with all bliss and beauty were the pair,
He passing glorious, she was heavenly fair.
Swiftly the seasons, winged with love, flew on,
And made her mother of a noble son,
The great MAINÁKA, who in triumph led
His Serpent beauties to the bridal bed;
And once when INDRA's might those pinions rent
That bare the swift hills through the firmament,
(So fierce his rage, no mountain could withstand
The wild bolt flashing from his red right hand,)
He fled to Ocean, powerful to save,
And hid his glory 'neath the friendly wave.

A gentle daughter came at length to bless
The royal mother with her loveliness;
Born once again, for in an earlier life
High fame was hers, as ŚIVA's faithful wife.

But her proud sire had dared the God to scorn;
Then was her tender soul with anguish torn,
And jealous for the lord she loved so well,
Her angered spirit left its mortal cell.
Now deigned the maid, a lovely boon, to spring
From that pure lady and the mountain-king.
When Industry and Virtue meet and kiss,
Holy their union, and the fruit is bliss.

Blest was that hour, and all the world was gay,
When MENÁ's daughter saw the light of day.
A rosy glow suffused the brightening sky;
An odorous breeze came sweeping softly by.
Breathed round the hill a sweet unearthly strain,
And the glad heavens poured down their flowery rain.

That fair young maiden diademmed with light
Made her dear mother's fame more sparkling bright,
As the blue offspring of the Turquois Hills
The parent mount with richer glory fills,
When the cloud's voice has caused the gem to spring,
Responsive to its gentle thundering.

Then was it sweet, as days flew by, to trace
The dawning charm of every infant grace,
Even as the crescent moons their glory pour
More full, more lovely than the eve before.

As yet the maiden was unknown to fame;
Child of the Mountain was her only name.

## UMÁ'S NATIVITY.

But when her mother, filled with anxious care
At her stern penance, cried Forbear! Forbear!
To a new title was the warning turned,
And UMÁ was the name the maiden earned.

    Loveliest was she of all his lovely race,
And dearest to her father.  On her face
Looking with love he ne'er could satisfy
The thirsty glances of a parent's eye.
When spring-tide bids a thousand flowerets bloom
Loading the breezes with their rich perfume,
Though here and there the wandering bee may rest,
He loves his own—his darling mango—best.
The Gods' bright river bathes with gold the skies,
And pure sweet eloquence adorns the wise.
The flambeau's glory is the shining fire;
She was the pride, the glory of her sire,
Shedding new lustre on his old descent,
His loveliest child, his richest ornament.

    The sparkling GANGÁ laved her heavenly home,
And o'er her islets would the maiden roam
Amid the dear companions of her play
With ball and doll to while the hours away.

    As swans in autumn in assembling bands
Fly back to GANGÁ's well-remembered sands:
As herbs beneath the darksome shades of night
Collect again their scattered rays of light:

So dawned upon the maiden's waking mind
The far-off memory of her life resigned,
And all her former learning in its train,
Feelings, and thoughts, and knowledge came again.
   Now beauty's prime, that craves no artful aid,
Ripened the loveliness of that young maid:
That needs no wine to fire the captive heart,—
The bow of Love without his flowery dart.
There was a glory beaming from her face,
With love's own light, and every youthful grace:
Ne'er had the painter's skilful hand portrayed
A lovelier picture than that gentle maid;
Ne'er sun-kissed lily more divinely fair
Unclosed her beauty to the morning air.
   Bright as a lotus, springing where she trod,
Her glowing feet shed radiance o'er the sod.
That arching neck, the step, the glance aside,
The proud swans taught her as they stemmed the tide,
Whilst of the maiden they would fondly learn
Her anklets' pleasant music in return.
   When the Almighty Maker first began
The marvellous beauty of that child to plan,
In full fair symmetry each rounded limb
Grew neatly fashioned and approved by Him:
The rest was faultless, for the Artist's care
Formed each young charm most excellently fair,

As if his moulding hand would fain express
The visible type of perfect loveliness.
   What thing of beauty may the poet dare
With the smooth wonder of those limbs compare?
The young tree springing by the brooklet's side?
The rounded trunk, the forest-monarch's pride?
Too rough that trunk, too cold that young tree's stem;
A softer, warmer thing must vie with them.
   Her hidden beauties though no tongue may tell,
Yet ŚIVA's love will aid the fancy well:
No other maid could deem her boasted charms
Worthy the clasp of such a husband's arms.
Between the partings of fair UMÁ's vest
Came hasty glimpses of a lovely breast:
So closely there the sweet twin hillocks rose,
Scarce could the lotus in the vale repose.
And if her loosened zone e'er slipped below,
All was so bright beneath the mantle's flow,
So dazzling bright, as if the maid had braced
A band of gems to sparkle round her waist;
And the dear dimples of her downy skin
Seemed fitting couch for Love to revel in.
Her arms were softer than the flowery dart,
Young KÁMA's arrow, that subdues the heart;
For vain his strife with ŚIVA, till at last
He chose those chains to bind his conqueror fast.

E'en the new moon poured down a paler beam
When her long fingers flashed their rosy gleam,
And brighter than Aśoka's blossom threw
A glory round, like summer's evening hue.
The strings of pearl across her bosom thrown
Increased its beauty, and enhanced their own,—
Her breast, her jewels seeming to agree,
The adorner now, and now the adorned to be.
When BEAUTY gazes on the fair full moon,
No lotus charms her, for it blooms at noon:
If on that flower she feed her raptured eye,
No moon is shining from the mid-day sky;
She looked on UMÁ's face, more heavenly fair,
And found their glories both united there.
The loveliest flower that ever opened yet
Laid in the fairest branch: a fair pearl set
In richest coral, with her smile might vie
Flashing through lips bright with their rosy dye.
And when she spoke, upon the maiden's tongue,
Distilling nectar, such rare accents hung,
The sweetest note that e'er the Koïl poured
Seemed harsh and tuneless as a jarring chord.
The melting glance of that soft liquid eye,
Tremulous like lilies when the breezes sigh,
Which learnt it first—so winning and so mild—
The gentle fawn, or MENÁ's gentler child?

And oh, the arching of her brow! so fine
Was the rare beauty of its pencilled line,
LOVE gazed upon her forehead in despair
And spurned the bow he once esteemed so fair:
Her long bright tresses too might shame the pride
Of envious yaks who roamed the mountain-side.
Surely the Maker's care had been to bring
From Nature's store each sweetest, loveliest thing,
As if the world's Creator would behold
All beauty centred in a single mould.

When holy NÁRAD—Saint who roams at will—
First saw the daughter of the royal hill,
He hailed the bride whom ŚIVA's love should own
Half of himself, and partner of his throne.
HIMÁLAYA listened, and the father's pride
Would yield the maiden for no other's bride:
To Fire alone of all bright things we raise
The holy hymn, the sacrifice of praise.
But still the monarch durst not, could not bring
His child, unsought, to Heaven's supremest King;
But as a good man fears his earnest prayer
Should rise unheeded, and with thoughtful care
Seeks for some friend his eager suit to aid,
Thus great HIMÁLAYA in his awe delayed.

Since the sad moment when his gentle bride
In the full glory of her beauty died,
The mournful Śiva in the holy grove
Had dwelt in solitude, and known not love.
High on that hill where musky breezes throw
Their balmy odours o'er eternal snow;
Where heavenly minstrels pour their notes divine,
And rippling Gangá laves the mountain pine,
Clad in a coat of skin all rudely wrought
He lived for prayer and solitary thought.
The faithful band that served the hermit's will
Lay in the hollows of the rocky hill,
Where from the clefts the dark bitumen flowed.
Tinted with mineral dyes their bodies glowed;
Clad in rude mantles of the birch-tree's rind,
With bright red garlands was their hair entwined.
The holy bull before his master's feet
Shook the hard-frozen earth with echoing feet,
And as he heard the lion's roaring swell
In distant thunder from the rocky dell,
In angry pride he raised his voice of fear
And from the mountain drove the startled deer.

Bright fire—a shape the God would sometimes wear
Who takes eight various forms—was glowing there.
Then the great deity who gives the prize
Of penance, prayer, and holy exercise,

As though to earn the meed he grants to man,
Himself the penance and the pain began.

　Now to that holy lord, to whom is given
Honour and glory by the Gods in heaven,
The worship of a gift HIMÁLAYA paid,
And towards his dwelling sent the lovely maid;
Her task, attended by her youthful train,
To woo his widowed heart to love again.


　The hermit welcomed with a courteous brow
That gentle enemy of hermit vow.
The still pure breast where Contemplation dwells
Defies the charmer and the charmer's spells.
Calm and unmoved he viewed the wondrous maid,
And bade her all his pious duties aid.
She culled fresh blossoms at the God's command,
Sweeping the altar with a careful hand;
The holy grass for sacred rites she sought,
And day by day the fairest water brought.
And if the unwonted labour caused a sigh,
The fair-haired lady turned her languid eye
Where the pale moon on ŚIVA's forehead gleamed,
And swift through all her frame returning vigour streamed.

## CANTO SECOND.

# Canto Second.

---o---

## *THE ADDRESS TO BRAHMÁ.*

WHILE impious TÁRAK in resistless might
Was troubling heaven and earth with wild affright,
To BRAHMÁ's high abode, by INDRA led,
The mournful deities for refuge fled.
As when the Day-God's loving beams awake
The lotus slumbering on the silver lake,
So BRAHMÁ deigned his glorious face to show,
And poured sweet comfort on their looks of woe.
  Then nearer came the suppliant Gods to pay
Honour to him whose face turns every way.
They bowed them low before the Lord of Speech,
And sought with truthful words his heart to reach:
"Glory to Thee! before the world was made,
One single form thy Majesty displayed.
Next Thou, to body forth the mystic Three,
Didst fill three Persons: Glory, Lord, to Thee!
Unborn and unbegotten! from thy hand
The fruitful seed rained down; at thy command

From that small germ o'er quickening waters thrown
All things that move not, all that move have grown.
Before thy triple form in awe they bow:
Maker, preserver, and destroyer, Thou!
Thou, when a longing urged thee to create,
Thy single form in twain didst separate.
The Sire, the Mother that made all things be
By their first union were but parts of Thee.
From them the life that fills this earthly frame,
And fruitful Nature, self-renewing, came.
Thou countest not thy time by mortals' light;
With Thee there is but one vast day and night.
When BRAHMÁ slumbers fainting Nature dies,
When BRAHMÁ wakens all again arise.
Creator of the world, and uncreate!
Endless! all things from Thee their end await.
Before the world wast Thou! each Lord shall fall
Before Thee, mightiest, highest, Lord of all.
Thy self-taught soul thine own deep spirit knows;
Made by thyself thy mighty form arose;
Into the same, when all things have their end,
Shall thy great self, absorbed in Thee, descend.
Lord, who may hope thy essence to declare?
Firm, yet as subtile as the yielding air:
Fixt, all-pervading; ponderous, yet light,
Patent to all, yet hidden from the sight.

Thine are the sacred hymns which mortals raise,
Commencing ever with the word of praise,
With three-toned chant the sacrifice to grace,
And win at last in heaven a blissful place.
They hail Thee Nature labouring to free
The Immortal Soul from low humanity;
Hail Thee the stranger Spirit, unimpressed,
Gazing on Nature from thy lofty rest.
Father of fathers, God of gods art thou,
Creator, highest, hearer of the vow!
Thou art the sacrifice, and Thou the priest,
Thou, he that eateth; Thou, the holy feast.
Thou art the knowledge which by Thee is taught,
The mighty thinker, and the highest thought!"

  Pleased with their truthful praise, his favouring eye
He turned upon the dwellers in the sky,
While from four mouths his words in gentle flow
Come welling softly to assuage their woe:
"Welcome! glad welcome, Princes! ye who hold
Your lofty sovereignties ordained of old.
But why so mournful? what has dimmed your light?
Why shine your faces less divinely bright?
Like stars that pour forth weaker, paler gleams,
When the fair moon with brighter radiance beams.

O say, in vain doth mighty INDRA bear
The thunderbolt of heaven, unused to spare?
VRITRA, the furious fiend, 'twas strong to slay:
Why dull and blunted is that might to-day?
See, VARUN'S noose hangs idly on his arm,
Like some fell serpent quelled by magic charm.
Weak is KUVERA's hand, his arm no more
Wields the dread mace it once so proudly bore;
But like a tree whose boughs are lopped away,
It tells of piercing woe, and dire dismay.
In days of yore how YAMA's sceptre shone!
Fled are its glories, all its terrors gone;
Despised and useless as a quenched brand,
All idly now it marks the yielding sand.
Fallen are the Lords of Light, ere now the gaze
Shrank from the coming of their fearful blaze;
So changed are they, the undazzled eye may see
Like pictured forms, each rayless deity.
Some baffling power has curbed the breezes' swell:
Vainly they chafe against the secret spell.
We know some barrier checks their wonted course,
When refluent waters seek again their source.
The RUDRAS too—fierce demigods who bear
The curved moon hanging from their twisted hair—
Tell by their looks of fear, and shame, and woe,
Of threats now silenced, of a mightier foe.

Glory and power, ye Gods, were yours of right:
Have ye now yielded to some stronger might,
Even as on earth a general law may be
Made powerless by a special text's decree?
Then say, my sons, why seek ye BRAHMÁ'S throne?
'Tis mine to frame the worlds, and yours to guard your
    own."

Then INDRA turned his thousand glorious eyes,
Glancing like lilies when the soft wind sighs,
And in the Gods' behalf, their mighty chief
Urged the Most Eloquent to tell their grief.
Then rose the heavenly Teacher, by whose side
Dim seemed the glories of the Thousand-eyed,
And with his hands outspread, to BRAHMÁ spake,
Couched on his own dear flower, the daughter of the lake:
" O mighty Being! surely thou dost know
The unceasing fury of our ruthless foe;
For thou canst see the secret thoughts that lie
Deep in the heart, yet open to thine eye.
The vengeful TÁRAK, in resistless might,
Like some dire Comet, gleaming wild affright,
O'er all the worlds an evil influence sheds,
And, in thy favour strong, destruction spreads.
All bow before him: on his palace wall
The sun's first ray and parting splendour fall;

Ne'er could he waken with a lovelier glance
His own dear lotus from her nightly trance.
For him, proud fiend, the moon no waning knows,
But with unminished full-orbed lustre glows.
Too faint for him the crescent glory set
Amid the blaze of ŚIVA's coronet.
How fair his garden, where the obedient breeze
Dares steal no blossom from the slumbering trees!
The wild wind checks his blustering pinions there,
And gently whispering fans the balmy air;
While through the inverted year the seasons pour,
To win the demon's grace, their flowery store.
For him, the River-god beneath the stream,
Marks the young pearl increase its silver gleam,
Until, its beauty and its growth complete,
He bears the offering to his master's feet.
The Serpents, led by VÁSUKI, their king,
Across his nightly path their lustre fling;
Bright as a torch their flashing jewels blaze,
Nor wind, nor rain, can dim their dazzling rays.
E'en INDRA, sovereign of the blissful skies,
To gain his love by flattering homage tries,
And sends him oft those flowers of wondrous hue
That on the heavenly tree in beauty grew.
Yet all these offerings brought from day to day,
This flattery, fail his ruthless hand to stay.

Earth, hell, and heaven, beneath his rage must groan,
Till force can hurl him from his evil throne.
Alas! where glowed the bright celestial bowers,
And gentle fair ones nursed the opening flowers,
Where heavenly trees a heavenly odour shed,
O'er a sad desert ruin reigns instead.
He roots up MERU's sacred peaks, where stray
The fiery coursers of the God of Day,
To form bright slopes, and glittering mounds of ease,
In the broad gardens of his palaces.
There, on his couch, the mighty lord is fanned
To sweetest slumber by a heavenly band;
Poor captive nymphs, who stand in anguish by,
Drop the big tear, and heave the ceaseless sigh.
And now have INDRA's elephants defiled
The sparkling stream where heavenly GANGÁ smiled,
And her gold lotuses the fiend has taken,
To deck his pools, and left her all forsaken.
The Gods of heaven no more delight to roam
O'er all the world, far from their glorious home.
They dread the demon's impious might, nor dare
Speed their bright chariots through the fields of air.
And when our worshippers in duty bring
The appointed victims for the offering,
He tears them from the flame with magic art,
While we all powerless watch with drooping heart.

He too has stolen from his master's side
The steed of heavenly race, great INDRA's pride.
No more our hosts, so glorious once, withstand
The fierce dominion of the demon's hand,
As herbs of healing virtue fail to tame
The sickness raging through the infected frame.
Idly the discus hangs on VISHṆU's neck,
And our last hope is vain, that it would check
The haughty TÁRAK's might, and flash afar
Ruin and death—the thunderbolt of war.
E'en INDRA's elephant has felt the might
Of his fierce monsters in the deadly fight,
Which spurn the dust in fury, and defy
The threatening clouds that sail along the sky.
Therefore, O Lord, we seek a chief, that he
May lead the hosts of heaven to victory,
Even as holy men who long to sever
The immortal spirit from its shell for ever,
Seek lovely Virtue's aid to free the soul
From earthly ties and action's base control.
Thus shall he save us: proudly will we go
Under his escort 'gainst the furious foe;
And INDRA, conqueror in turn, shall bring
FORTUNE, dear captive, home with joy and triumphing."

Sweet as the rains—the fresh'ning rains—that pour
On the parched earth when thunders cease to roar,

Were BRAHMÁ's words: "Gods, I have heard your grief;
Wait ye in patience: time will bring relief.
'Tis not for me, my children, to create
A chief to save you from your mournful fate.
Not by my hand the fiend must be destroyed,
For my kind favour has he once enjoyed;
And well ye know that e'en a poisonous tree
By him who planted it unharmed should be.
He sought it eagerly, and long ago
I gave my favour to your demon-foe,
And stayed his awful penance, that had hurled
Flames, death, and ruin o'er the subject world.
When that great warrior battles for his life,
O, who may conquer in the deadly strife,
Save one of ŚIVA's seed ? He is the light,
Reigning supreme beyond the depths of night.
Nor I, nor VISHṆU, his full power may share,
Lo, where he dwells in solitude and prayer!
Go, seek the Hermit in the grove alone,
And to the God be UMÁ's beauty shown.
Perchance, the Mountain-child, with magnet's force,
May turn the iron from its steadfast course,
Bride of the mighty God; for only she
Can bear to Him as water bears to me.
Then from their love a mighty Child shall rise,
And lead to war the armies of the skies.

Freed by his hand, no more the heavenly maids
Shall twine their glittering hair in mournful braids."

He spake, and vanished from their wondering sight;
And they sped homeward to their world of light.
But INDRA, still on BRAHMÁ's words intent,
To KÁMA's dwelling-place his footsteps bent.
Swiftly he came: the yearning of his will
Made INDRA's lightning course more speedy still.
The LOVE-GOD, armed with flowers divinely sweet,
In lowly homage bowed before his feet.
Around his neck, where bright love-tokens clung,
Arched like a maiden's brow, his bow was hung,
And blooming SPRING, his constant follower, bore
The mango twig, his weapon famed of yore.

## CANTO THIRD.

# Canto Third.

---o---

## THE DEATH OF LOVE.

IN eager gaze the sovereign of the skies
Looked full on KÁMA with his thousand eyes:
E'en such a gaze as trembling suppliants bend,
When danger threatens, on a mighty friend.

   Close by his side, where INDRA bade him rest,
The LOVE-GOD sate, and thus his lord addressed:
" All-knowing INDRA, deign, my Prince, to tell
Thy heart's desire in earth, or heaven, or hell:
Double the favour, mighty sovereign, thou
Hast thought on KÁMA, O, command him now!
Who angers thee by toiling for the prize,
By penance, prayer, or holy sacrifice?
What mortal being dost thou count thy foe?
Speak, I will tame him with my darts and bow.
Has some one feared the endless change of birth,
And sought the path that leads the soul from earth?
Slave to a glancing eye thy foe shall bow,
And own the witchery of a woman's brow;

E'en though the object of thine envious rage
Were taught high wisdom by the immortal sage,
With billowy passions will I whelm his soul,
Like rushing waves that spurn the bank's control.
Or has the ripe full beauty of a spouse,
Too fondly faithful to her bridal vows,
Ravished thy spirit from thee?   Thine, all thine
Around thy neck her loving arms shall twine.
Has thy love, jealous of another's charms,
Spurned thee in wrath when flying to her arms?
I'll rack her yielding bosom with such pain,
Soon shall she be all love and warmth again,
And wildly fly in fevered haste to rest
Her aching heart close, close to thy dear breast.
Lay, INDRA, lay thy threatening bolt aside:
My gentle darts shall tame the haughtiest pride,
And all that war with heaven and thee shall know
The magic influence of thy KÁMA's bow;
For woman's curling lip shall bow them down,
Fainting in terror at her threatening frown.
Flowers are my arms, mine only warrior SPRING,
Yet in thy favour am I strong, great King.
What can their strength who draw the bow avail
Against my matchless power when I assail?
Strong is the Trident-bearing God, yet he,
The mighty ŚIVA, e'en, must yield to me."

Then INDRA answered with a dawning smile,
Resting his foot upon a stool the while:
"Dear God of Love, thou truly hast displayed
The power unrivalled of thy promised aid.
My hope is all in thee: my weapons are
The thunderbolt and thou, more mighty far.
But vain, all vain the bolt of heaven to fright
Those holy Saints whom penance arms aright.
Thy power exceeds all bound: thou, only thou,
All-conquering Deity, canst help me now!
Full well I know thy nature, and assign
This toil to thee, which needs a strength like thine:
As on that snake alone will KRISHNA rest,
That bears the earth upon his haughty crest.
Our task is well-nigh done: thy boasted dart
Has power to conquer even ŚIVA's heart.
Hear what the Gods, oppressed with woe, would fain
From mighty ŚIVA through thine aid obtain.
He may beget—and none in heaven but he—
A chief to lead our hosts to victory.
But all his mind with holiest lore is fraught,
Bent on the Godhead is his every thought.
Thy darts, O LOVE, alone can reach him now,
And lure his spirit from the hermit vow.
Go, seek HIMÁLAYA's Mountain-child, and aid
With all thy loveliest charms the lovely maid,

So may she please his fancy: only she
May wed with Śiva: such the fixt decree.
E'en now my bands of heavenly maids have spied
Fair Umá dwelling by the Hermit's side.
There by her father's bidding rests she still,
Sweet minister, upon the cold bleak hill.
Go, Káma, go! perform this great emprise,
And free from fear the Rulers of the Skies;
We need thy favour, as the new-sown grain
Calls for the influence of the gentle rain.
Go, Káma, go! thy flowery darts shall be
Crowned with success o'er this great deity.
Yea, and thy task is e'en already done,
For praise and glory are that instant won
When a bold heart dares manfully essay
The deed which others shrink from in dismay.
Gods are thy suppliants, Káma, and on thee
Depends the triple world's security.
No cruel deed will stain thy flowery bow:
With all thy gentlest, mightiest valour, go!
And now, Disturber of the spirit, see
Spring, thy beloved, will thy comrade be,
And gladly aid thee Śiva's heart to tame:
None bids the whispering Wind, and yet he fans the flame."

He spake, and Káma bowed his bright head down,
And took his bidding like a flowery crown.

Above his wavy curls great INDRA bent,
And fondly touched his soldier ere he went,
With that hard hand—but, O, how gentle now!—
That fell so heavy on his elephant's brow.
   Then for that snow-crowned hill he turned away,
Where all alone the heavenly Hermit lay.
His fearful RATI and his comrade SPRING
Followed the guidance of Love's mighty king.
There will he battle in unwonted strife,
Return a conqueror or be reft of life.

   How fair was SPRING! To fill the heart with
      love,
And lure the Hermit from his thoughts above,
In that pure grove he grew so heavenly bright
That KÁMA's envy wakened at the sight.
   Now the bright Day-God turned his burning ray
To where KUVERA holds his royal sway,
While the sad South in whispering breezes sighed
And mourned his absence like a tearful bride.
Then from its stem the red Aśoka threw
Full buds and flowerets of celestial hue,
Nor waited for the maiden's touch, the sweet
Beloved pressure of her tinkling feet.
There grew LOVE's arrow, his dear mango spray,
Winged with young leaves to speed its airy way,

And at the call of SPRING the wild bees came,
Grouping the syllables of KÁMA's name.
How sighed the spirit o'er that loveliest flower
That boasts no fragrance to enrich its dower!
For Nature, wisest mother, oft prefers
To part more fairly those good gifts of hers.
There from the tree Palása blossoms spread,
Curved like the crescent moon, their rosiest red,
With opening buds that looked as if young SPRING
Had pressed his nails there in his dallying:
Sweet wanton SPRING, to whose enchanting face
His flowery Tilaka gave fairer grace:
Who loves to tint his lip, the mango spray,
With the fresh colours of the early day,
And powder its fine red with many a bee
That sips the oozing nectar rapturously.
The cool gale speeding o'er the shady lawns
Shook down the sounding leaves, while startled fawns
Ran wildly at the viewless foe, all blind
With pollen wafted by the fragrant wind.
Sweet was the Köil's voice, his neck still red
With mango buds on which he late had fed:
'Twas as the voice of LOVE to bid the dame
Spurn her cold pride, nor quench the gentle flame.
What though the heat has stained the tints that dyed
With marvellous bloom the heavenly minstrel's bride?

Neither her smile nor sunny glances fail:
Bright is her lip, although her cheek be pale.
E'en the pure hermits owned the secret power
Of warm SPRING coming in unwonted hour,
While LOVE's delightful witchery gently stole
With strong sweet influence o'er the saintly soul.

On came the Archer-God, and at his side
The timid RATI, his own darling bride,
While breathing nature showed how deep it felt,
At passion's glowing touch, the senses melt.
For there in eager love the wild bee dipp'd
In the dark flower-cup where his partner sipp'd.
Here in the shade the hart his horn declined,
And, while joy closed her eyes, caressed the hind.
There from her trunk the elephant had poured
A lily-scented stream to cool her lord,
While the fond love-bird by the silver flood
Gave to his mate the tasted lotus bud.
Full in his song the minstrel stayed to sip
The heavenlier nectar of his darling's lip.
Pure pearls of heat had late distained the dye,
But flowery wine was sparkling in her eye.
How the young creeper's beauty charmed the
    view,
Fair as the fairest maid, as playful too!

Here some bright blossoms, lovelier than the rest,
In full round beauty matched her swelling breast.
Here in a thin bright line, some delicate spray,
Red as her lip, ravished the soul away.
And then how loving, and how close they clung
To the tall trees that fondly o'er them hung!
Bright, heavenly wantons poured the witching strain,
Quiring for ŚIVA'S ear, but all in vain.
No charmer's spell may check the firm control
Won by the holy o'er the impassioned soul.

   The Hermit's servant hasted to the door:
In his left hand a branch of gold he bore.
He touched his lip for silence: " Peace! be still!
Nor mar the quiet of this holy hill."
He spake: no dweller of the forest stirred,
No wild bee murmured, hushed was every bird.
Still and unmoved, as in a picture stood
All life that breathed within the waving wood.

   As some great monarch when he goes to war
Shuns the fierce aspect of a baleful star,
So KÁMA hid him from the Hermit's eye,
And sought a path that led unnoticed by,
Where tangled flowers and clustering trailers spread
Their grateful canopy o'er ŚIVA'S head.
Bent on his hardy enterprise, with awe
The Three-eyed Lord—great Penitent—he saw.

There sate the God beneath a pine-tree's shade,
Where on a mound a tiger's skin was laid.
Absorbed in holiest thought, erect and still,
The Hermit rested on the gentle hill.
His shoulders drooping down, each foot was bent
Beneath the body of the Penitent.
With open palms the hands were firmly pressed,
As though a lotus lay upon his breast.
A double rosary in each ear, behind
With wreathing serpents were his locks entwined.
His coat of hide shone blacker to the view
Against his neck of brightly beaming blue.
How wild the look, how terrible the frown
Of his dark eyebrows bending sternly down!
How fiercely glared his eyes' unmoving blaze
Fixed in devotion's meditating gaze!
Calm as a full cloud resting on a hill,
A waveless lake when every breeze is still,
Like a torch burning in a sheltered spot,
So still was He, unmoving, breathing not.

 So full the stream of marvellous glory poured
From the bright forehead of that mighty Lord,
Pale seemed the crescent moon upon his head,
And slenderer than a slender lotus thread.
At all the body's nine-fold gates of sense
He had barred in the pure Intelligence,

To ponder on the Soul which sages call
Eternal Spirit, highest, over all.

 How sad was KÁMA at the awful sight,
How failed his courage in a swoon of fright!
As near and nearer to the God he came
Whom wildest thought could never hope to tame,
Unconsciously his hands, in fear and woe,
Dropped the sweet arrows and his flowery bow.
 But UMÁ came with all her maiden throng,
And KÁMA'S fainting heart again was strong;
Bright flowers of spring, in every lovely hue,
Around the lady's form rare beauty threw.
Some clasped her neck like strings of purest pearls,
Some shot their glory through her wavy curls.
Bending her graceful head as half-oppressed
With swelling charms even too richly blest,
Fancy might deem that beautiful young maiden
Some slender tree with its sweet flowers o'erladen.
From time to time her gentle hand replaced
The flowery girdle slipping from her waist:
It seemed that LOVE could find no place more fair,
So hung his newest, dearest bowstring there.
A greedy bee kept hovering round to sip
The fragrant nectar of her blooming lip.
She closed her eyes in terror of the thief,
And beat him from her with a lotus leaf.

The angry curl of RATI's lip confessed
The shade of envy that stole o'er her breast.
Through KÁMA's soul fresh hope and courage flew,
As that sweet vision blessed his eager view.
So bright, so fair, so winning soft was she,
Who could not conquer in such company?

   Now UMÁ came, fair maid, his destined bride,
With timid steps approaching ŚIVA's side.
In contemplation will he brood no more,
He sees the Godhead, and his task is o'er.
He breathes, he moves, the earth begins to rock,
The Snake, her bearer, trembling at the shock.
   Due homage then his own dear servant paid,
And told him of the coming of the maid.
He learnt his Master's pleasure by the nod,
And led HIMÁLAYA's daughter to the God.
Before his feet her young companions spread
Fresh leaves and blossoms as they bowed the head,
While UMÁ stooped so low, that from her hair
Dropped the bright flower that starred the midnight
      there.
To him whose ensign bears the bull she bent,
Till each spray fell, her ear's rich ornament.
"Sweet maid," cried ŚIVA, "surely thou shalt be
Blessed with a husband who loves none but thee!"

Her fear was banished, and her hope was high:
A God had spoken, and Gods cannot lie.

Rash as some giddy moth that wooes the flame,
LOVE seized the moment, and prepared to aim.
Close by the daughter of the Mountain-King,
He looked on ŚIVA, and he eyed his string.
While with her radiant hand fair UMÁ gave
A rosary, of the lotuses that lave
Their beauties in the heavenly GANGÁ'S wave,
And the great Three-Eyed God was fain to take
The offering for the well-loved suppliant's sake,
On his bright bow LOVE placed the unerring dart,
The soft beguiler of the stricken heart.
Like the Moon's influence on the sea at rest,
Came passion stealing o'er the Hermit's breast,
While on the maiden's lip that mocked the dye
Of ripe red fruit, he bent his melting eye.
And oh! how showed the lady's love for him,
The heaving bosom, and each quivering limb!
Like young Kadambas, when the leaf-buds swell,
At the warm touch of Spring they love so well.
But still, with downcast eyes, she sought the ground,
And durst not turn their burning glances round.
Then with strong effort, ŚIVA lulled to rest,
The storm of passion in his troubled breast,

And seeks, with angry eyes that round him roll,
Whence came the tempest o'er his tranquil soul.
He looked, and saw the bold young archer stand,
His bow bent ready in his skilful hand,
Drawn towards the eye; his shoulder well depressed,
And the left foot thrown forward as a rest.

Then was the Hermit-God to madness lashed,
Then from his eye red flames of fury flashed.
So changed the beauty of that glorious brow,
Scarce could the gaze support its terror now.

Hark! heavenly voices sighing through the air:
" Be calm, great ŚIVA, O be calm and spare!"
Alas! that angry eye's resistless flashes
Have scorched the gentle King of Love to ashes!

But RATI saw not, for she swooned away;
Senseless and breathless on the earth she lay;
Sleep while thou mayst, unconscious lady, sleep!
Soon wilt thou rise to sigh and wake to weep.

E'en as the red bolt rives the leafy bough,
So ŚIVA smote the hinderer of his vow;
Then fled with all his train to some lone place
Far from the witchery of a female face.

Sad was HIMÁLAYA's daughter: grief and shame
O'er the young spirit of the maiden came:

Grief—for she loved, and all her love was vain ;
Shame—she was spurned before her youthful train.
She turned away, with fear and woe oppressed,
To hide her sorrow on her father's breast;
Then, in the fond arms of her pitying sire,
Closed her sad eyes for fear of ŚIVA's ire.
Still in his grasp the weary maiden lay,
While he sped swiftly on his homeward way.

   Thus have I seen the elephant stoop to drink,
And lift a lily from the fountain's brink.
Thus, when he rears his mighty head on high,
Across his tusks I've seen that lily lie.

# CANTO FOURTH.

# Canto Fourth.

### *RATI'S LAMENT.*

Sad, solitary, helpless, faint, forlorn,
Woke Káma's darling from her swoon to mourn.
Too soon her gentle soul returned to know
The pangs of widowhood—that word of woe.
Scarce could she raise her, trembling, from the ground,
Scarce dared to bend her anxious gaze around,
Unconscious yet those greedy eyes should never
Feed on his beauty more—gone, gone for ever.

" Speak to me, Káma ! why so silent ? give
One word in answer—doth my Káma live ? "
There on the turf his dumb cold ashes lay,
Whose soul that fiery flash had scorched away.
She clasped the dank earth in her wild despair,
Her bosom stained, and rent her long bright hair,
Till hill and valley caught the mourner's cry,
And pitying breezes echoed sigh for sigh.

"Oh thou wast beautiful: fond lovers sware
Their own bright darlings were like KÁMA, fair.
Sure woman's heart is stony: can it be
That I still live while this is all of thee?
Where art thou, KÁMA?  Could my dearest leave
His own fond RATI here alone to grieve?
So must the sad forsaken lotus die
When her bright river leaves his channel dry.
KÁMA, dear KÁMA, call again to mind
How thou wast ever gentle, I was kind.
Let not my prayer, thy RATI's prayer, be vain;
Come as of old, and bless these eyes again!
Wilt thou not hear me? Think of those sweet hours
When I would bind thee with my zone of flowers,
Those soft gay fetters o'er thee fondly wreathing,
Thine only punishment when gently breathing
In tones of love thy heedless sigh betrayed
The name, dear traitor! of some rival maid.
Then would I pluck a floweret from my tress
And beat thee till I forced thee to confess,
While in my play the falling leaves would cover
The eyes—the bright eyes—of my captive lover.
And then those words that made me, oh, so blest—
"Dear love, thy home is in my faithful breast!"
Alas, sweet words, too blissful to be true,
Or how couldst thou have died, nor RATI perish too?

Yes, I will fly to thee, of thee bereft,
And leave this world which thou, my life, hast left.
Cold, gloomy, now this wretched world must be,
For all its pleasures came from only thee.
When night has veiled the city in its shade,
Thou, only thou, canst soothe the wandering maid,
And guide her trembling at the thunder's roar
Safe through the darkness to her lover's door.
In vain the wine-cup, as it circles by,
Lisps in her tongue and sparkles in her eye.
Long locks are streaming, and the cheek glows red:
But all is mockery, LOVE—dear LOVE—is dead.
The MOON, sweet spirit, shall lament for thee,
Late, dim, and joyless shall his rising be.
Days shall fly on, and he forget to take
His full bright glory, mourning for thy sake.
Say, KÁMA, say, whose arrow now shall be
The soft green shoot of thy dear mango tree,
The favourite spray which Köils love so well,
And praise in sweetest strain its wondrous spell?
This line of bees which strings thy useless bow
Hums mournful echo to my cries of woe.
Come in thy lovely shape and teach again
The Köil's mate, that knows the tender strain,
Her gentle task to waft to longing ears
The lover's hope, the distant lover's fears.

Come, bring once more that ecstasy of bliss,
The fond dear look, the smile, and ah! that kiss!
Fainting with woe, my soul refuses rest
When memory pictures how I have been blest.
See, thou didst weave a garland, love, to deck
With all spring's fairest buds thy RATI's neck.
Sweet are those flowers as they were culled to-day,
And is my KÁMA's form more frail than they?
His pleasant task my lover had begun,
But stern Gods took him ere the work was done;
Return, my KÁMA, at thy RATI's cry,
And stain this foot which waits the rosy dye.

 Now will I hie me to the fatal pile,
And ere heaven's maids have hailed thee with a smile,
Or on my love their winning glances thrown,
I will be there, and claim thee for mine own.
Yet though I come, my lasting shame will be
That I have lived one moment after thee.
Ah, how shall I thy funeral rites prepare,
Gone soul and body to the viewless air?
With thy dear SPRING I've seen thee talk and smile,
Shaping an arrow for thy bow the while.
Where is he now, thy darling friend, the giver
Of many a bright sweet arrow for thy quiver?
Is he too sent upon death's dreary path,
Scorched by the cruel God's inexorable wrath?"

Stricken in spirit by her cries of woe,
Like venomed arrows from a mighty bow,
A moment fled, and gentle SPRING was there,
To ask her grief, to soothe her wild despair.
She beat her breast more wildly than before,
With greater floods her weeping eyes ran o'er.
When friends are nigh the spirit finds relief
In the full gushing torrent of its grief.

" Turn, gentle friend, thy weeping eyes, and see
That dear companion who was all to me.
His crumbling dust with which the breezes play,
Bearing it idly in their course away,
White as the silver feathers of a dove,
Is all that's left me of my murdered love.
    Now come, my KÁMA. SPRING, who was so dear,
Longs to behold thee. Oh, appear, appear!
Fickle to women LOVE perchance may bend
His ear to listen to a faithful friend.
Remember, he walked ever at thy side
O'er bloomy meadows in the warm spring-tide,
That Gods above, and men, and fiends below
Should own the empire of thy mighty bow,
That ruthless bow, which pierces to the heart,
Strung with a lotus-thread, a flower its dart.

As dies a torch when winds sweep roughly by,
So is my light for ever fled, and I,
The lamp his cheering rays no more illume,
Am wrapt in darkness, misery and gloom.
Fate took my love, and spared the widow's breath,
Yet fate is guilty of a double death.
When the wild monster tramples on the ground
The tree some creeper garlands closely round,
Reft of the guardian which it thought so true,
Forlorn and withered, it must perish too.
Then come, dear friend, the true one's pile prepare,
And send me quickly to my husband there.
Call it not vain: the mourning lotus dies
When the bright MOON, her lover, quits the skies.
When sinks the red cloud in the purple west,
Still clings his bride, the lightning, to his breast.
All nature keeps the eternal high decree:
Shall woman fail? I come, my love, to thee!

 Now on the pile my faint limbs will I throw,
Clasping his ashes, lovely even so,—
As if beneath my weary frame were spread
Soft leaves and blossoms for a flowery bed.
And oh, dear comrade (for in happier hours
Oft have I heaped a pleasant bed of flowers
For thee and him beneath the spreading tree),
Now quickly raise the pile for LOVE and me.

And in thy mercy gentle breezes send
To fan the flame that wafts away thy friend,
And shorten the sad moments that divide
Impatient KÁMA from his RATI's side;
Set water near us in a single urn,
We'll sip in heaven from the same in turn;
And let thine offering to his spirit be
Sprays fresh and lovely from the mango tree,
Culled when the round young buds begin to swell,
For KÁMA loved those fragrant blossoms well."

As RATI thus complained in faithful love,
A heavenly voice breathed round her from above,
Falling in pity like the gentle rain
That brings the dying herbs to life again:
" Bride of the flower-armed God, thy lord shall be
Not ever distant, ever deaf to thee.
Give me thine ear, sad lady, I will tell
Why perished KÁMA, whom thou lovedst well.
The Lord of Life in every troubled sense
Too warmly felt his fair child's influence.
He quenched the fire, but mighty vengeance came
On KÁMA, fanner of the unholy flame.
When ŚIVA by her penance won has led
HIMÁLAYA's daughter to her bridal bed,

His bliss to KÁMA shall the God repay,
And give again the form he snatched away.
Thus did the gracious God, at JUSTICE' prayer,
The term of LOVE's sad punishment declare.
The Gods, like clouds, are fierce and gentle too,
Now hurl the bolt, now drop sweet heavenly dew.
Live, widowed lady, for thy lover's arms
Shall clasp again—oh, fondly clasp—thy charms.
In summer-heat the streamlet dies away
Beneath the fury of the God of Day:
Then, in due season, comes the pleasant rain,
And all is fresh, and fair, and full again."

 Thus breathed the spirit from the viewless air,
And stilled the raging of her wild despair;
While SPRING consoled with every soothing art,
Cheered by that voice from heaven, the mourner's heart,
Who watched away the hours, so sad and slow,
That brought the limit of her weary woe,
As the pale moon, quenched by the conquering light
Of garish day, longs for its own dear night.

## CANTO FIFTH.

# Canto Fifth.

―o―

## UMÁ'S REWARD.

Now woe to UMÁ, for young LOVE is slain,
Her Lord hath left her, and her hope is vain.
Woe, woe to UMÁ! how the Mountain-Maid
Cursed her bright beauty for its feeble aid!
'Tis Beauty's guerdon which she loves the best,
To bless her lover, and in turn be blest.
   Penance must aid her now—or how can she
Win the cold heart of that stern deity?
Penance, long penance: for that power alone
Can make such love, so high a Lord, her own.

   But, ah! how troubled was her mother's brow
At the sad tidings of the mourner's vow!
She threw her arms around her own dear maid,
Kissed, fondly kissed her, sighed, and wept, and prayed:
   " Are there no Gods, my child, to love thee here?
Frail is thy body, yet thy vow severe.

The lily, by the wild bee scarcely stirred,
Bends, breaks, and dies beneath the weary bird."
  Fast fell her tears, her prayer was strong, but still
That prayer was weaker than her daughter's will.
Who can recall the torrent's headlong force,
Or the bold spirit in its destined course?
  She sent a maiden to her sire, and prayed
He for her sake would grant some bosky shade,
That she might dwell in solitude, and there
Give all her soul to penance and to prayer.
In gracious love the great HIMÁLAYA smiled,
And did the bidding of his darling child.
Then to that hill which peacocks love she came,
Known to all ages by the lady's name.

  Still to her purpose resolutely true,
Her string of noble pearls aside she threw,
Which, slipping here and there, had rubbed away
The sandal dust that on her bosom lay,
And clad her in a hermit coat of bark,
Rough to her gentle limbs, and gloomy dark,
Pressing too tightly, till her swelling breast
Broke into freedom through the unwonted vest.
Her matted hair was full as lovely now
As when 'twas braided o'er her polished brow.

Thus the sweet beauties of the lotus shine
When bees festoon it in a graceful line;
And, though the tangled weeds that crown the rill
Cling o'er it closely, it is lovely still.
With zone of grass the votaress was bound,
Which reddened the fair form it girdled round:
Never before the lady's waist had felt
The ceaseless torment of so rough a belt.

Alas! her weary vow has caused to fade
The lovely colours that adorned the maid.
Pale is her hand, and her long finger-tips
Steal no more splendour from her paler lips,
Or, from the ball which in her play would rest,
Made bright and fragrant, on her perfumed breast.
Rough with the sacred grass those hands must be,
And worn with resting on her rosary.
Cold earth her couch, her canopy the skies,
Pillowed upon her arm the lady lies:
She who before was wont to rest her head
In the soft luxury of a sumptuous bed,
Vext by no troubles as she slumbered there,
But sweet flowers slipping from her loosened hair.
The maid put off, but only for awhile,
Her passioned glances and her witching smile.
She lent the fawn her moving, melting gaze,
And the fond creeper all her winning ways.

The trees that blossomed on that lonely mount
She watered daily from the neighbouring fount:
If she had been their nursing mother, she
Could not have tended them more carefully.
Not e'en her boy—her own bright boy—shall stay
Her love for them: her first dear children they.
Her gentleness had made the fawns so tame,
To her kind hand for fresh sweet grain they came,
And let the maid before her friends compare
Her own with eyes that shone as softly there.

   Then came the hermits of the holy wood
To see the votaress in her solitude;
Grey elders came; though young the maid might seem,
Her perfect virtue must command esteem.
They found her resting in that lonely spot,
The fire was kindled, and no rite forgot.
In hermit's mantle was she clad; her look
Fixt in deep thought upon the Holy Book.
So pure that grove: all war was made to cease,
And savage monsters lived in love and peace.
Pure was that grove: each newly built abode
Had leafy shrines where fires of worship glowed.

   But far too mild her penance, UMÁ thought,
To win from heaven the lordly meed she sought.

She would not spare her form, so fair and frail,
If sterner penance could perchance prevail.
Oft had sweet pastime wearied her, and yet
Fain would she match in toil the anchoret.
Sure the soft lotus at her birth had lent
Dear Umá's form its gentle element;
But gold, commingled with her being, gave
That will so strong, so beautifully brave.

Full in the centre of four blazing piles
Sate the fair lady of the winning smiles,
While on her head the mighty God of Day
Shot all the fury of his summer ray;
Yet her fixt gaze she turned upon the skies,
And quenched his splendour with her brighter eyes.
To that sweet face, though scorched by rays from heaven,
Still was the beauty of the lotus given,
Yet, worn by watching, round those orbs of light
A blackness gathered like the shades of night.
She cooled her dry lips in the bubbling stream,
And lived on Amrit from the pale moon-beam,
Sometimes in hunger culling from the tree
The rich ripe fruit that hung so temptingly.

Scorched by the fury of the noon-tide rays,
And fires that round her burned with ceaseless blaze,
Summer passed o'er her: rains of Autumn came
And throughly drenched the lady's tender frame.

So steams the earth, when mighty torrents pour
On thirsty fields all dry and parched before.
The first clear rain-drops falling on her brow,
Gem it one moment with their light, and now
Kissing her sweet lip find a welcome rest
In the deep valley of the lady's breast;
Then wander broken by the fall within
The mazy channels of her dimpled skin.
There as she lay upon her rocky bed,
No sumptuous roof above her gentle head,
Dark Night, her only witness, turned her eyes,
Red lightnings flashing from the angry skies,
And gazed upon her voluntary pain,
In wind, in sleet, in thunder, and in rain.
Still lay the maiden on the cold damp ground,
Though blasts of winter hurled their snows around,
Still pitying in her heart the mournful fate
Of those poor birds, so fond, so desolate,—
Doomed, hapless pair, to list each other's moan
Through the long hours of night, sad and alone.

 Chilled by the rain, the tender lotus sank:
She filled its place upon the streamlet's bank.
Sweet was her breath as when that lovely flower
Sheds its best odour in still evening's hour.
Red as its leaves her lips of coral hue:
Red as those quivering leaves they quivered too.

Of all stern penance it is called the chief
To nourish life upon the fallen leaf.
But even this the ascetic maiden spurned,
And for all time a glorious title earned.
APARNÁ—Lady of the unbroken fast—
Have sages called her, saints who knew the past.
Fair as the lotus fibres, soft as they,
In these stern vows she passed her night and day.
No mighty anchoret had e'er essayed
The ceaseless penance of this gentle maid.

There came a hermit: reverend was he
As Bráhmanhood's embodied sanctity.
With coat of skin, with staff and matted hair,
His face was radiant, and he spake her fair.
Up rose the maid the holy man to greet,
And humbly bowed before the hermit's feet.
Though meditation fill the pious breast,
It finds a welcome for a glorious guest:
 The sage received the honour duly paid,
And fixed his earnest gaze upon the maid.
While through her frame unwonted vigour ran,
Thus, in his silver speech, the blameless saint began:
"How can thy tender frame, sweet lady, bear
In thy firm spirit's task its fearful share?
Canst thou the grass and fuel duly bring,
And still unwearied seek the freshening spring?

Say, do the creeper's slender shoots expand,
Seeking each day fresh water from thy hand,
Till like thy lip each ruddy tendril glows,
That lip which, faded, still outreds the rose ?
With loving glance the timid fawns draw nigh :
Say dost thou still with joy their wants supply ?
For thee, O lotus-eyed, their glances shine,
Mocking the brightness of each look of thine.
O Mountain-Lady, it is truly said
That heavenly charms to sin have never led,
For even penitents may learn of thee
How pure, how gentle Beauty's self may be.
Bright GANGÁ falling with her heavenly waves,
HIMÁLAYA'S head with sacred water laves,
Bearing the flowers the seven great Sages fling
To crown the forehead of the Mountain-King.
Yet do thy deeds, O bright-haired maiden, shed
A richer glory round his awful head.
Purest of motives, Duty leads thy heart :
Pleasure and gain therein may claim no part.
O noble maid, the wise have truly said
That friendship soon in gentle heart is bred.
Seven steps together bind the lasting tie :
Then bend on me, dear Saint, a gracious eye.
Fain, lovely UMÁ, would a Bráhman learn
What noble guerdon would thy penance earn.

Say, art thou toiling for a second birth,
Where dwells the great Creator ?   O'er the earth
Resistless sway ?   Or fair as Beauty's Queen,
Peerless, immortal, shall thy form be seen ?

   The lonely soul bowed down by grief and pain,
By penance' aid some gracious boon may gain.
But what, O faultless one, can move thy heart
To dwell in solitude and prayer apart ?
Why should the cloud of grief obscure thy brow,
'Mid all thy kindred, who so loved as thou ?
Foes hast thou none : for what rash hand would dare
From serpent's head the magic gem to tear ?
Why dost thou seek the hermit's garb to try,
Thy silken raiment and thy gems thrown by ?
As though the sun his glorious state should leave,
Rayless to harbour 'mid the shades of eve.
Wouldst thou win heaven by thy holy spells ?
Already with the Gods thy father dwells.
A husband, lady ?   O forbear the thought,
A priceless jewel seeks not, but is sought.
Maiden, thy deep sighs tell me it is so ;
Yet, doubtful still, my spirit seeks to know
Couldst thou e'er love in vain ?   What heart so cold
That hath not eagerly its worship told ?
Ah ! could the cruel loved one, thou fair maid,
Look with cold glances on that bright hair's braid ?

Thy locks are hanging loosely o'er thy brow,
Thine ear is shaded by no lotus now.
See, where the sun hath scorched that tender neck
Which precious jewels once were proud to deck.
Still gleams the line where they were wont to
    cling,
As faintly shows the moon's o'ershadowed ring.
Now sure thy loved one, vain in beauty's pride,
Dreamed of himself when wandering at thy side,
Or he would count him blest to be the mark
Of that dear eye, so soft, so lustrous dark.
But, gentle UMÁ, let thy labour cease;
Turn to thy home, fair Saint, and rest in peace.
By many a year of penance duly done
Rich store of merit has my labour won.
Take then the half, thy secret purpose name;
Nor in stern hardships wear thy tender frame."

    The holy Bráhman ceased: but UMÁ's breast
In silence heaved, by love and fear opprest.
In mute appeal she turned her languid eye,
Darkened with weeping, not with softening dye,
To bid her maiden's friendly tongue declare
The cherished secret of her deep despair:
" Hear, holy Father, if thou still wouldst know,
Why her frail form endures this pain and woe,

As the soft lotus makes a screen to stay
The noontide fury of the God of Day.
Proudly disdaining all the blest above,
With heart and soul she seeks for Śiva's love.
For him alone, the Trident-wielding God,
The thorny paths of penance hath she trod.
But since that mighty one hath Káma slain,
Vain every hope, and every effort vain.
E'en as life fled, a keen but flowery dart
Young Love, the Archer, aimed at Śiva's heart.
The God in anger hurled the shaft away,
But deep in Umá's tender soul it lay;
Alas, poor maid! she knows no comfort now,
Her soul's on fire, her wild locks hide her brow.
She quits her father's halls, and frenzied roves
The icy mountain and the lonely groves.
Oft as the maidens of the minstrel throng
To hymn great Śiva's praises raised the song,
The lovelorn lady's sobs and deep-drawn sighs
Drew tears of pity from their gentle eyes.
Wakeful and fevered in the dreary night
Scarce closed her eyes, and then in wild affright
Rang through the halls her very bitter cry,
"God of the azure neck, why dost thou fly?"
While their soft bands her loving arms would cast
Round the dear vision fading all too fast.

Her skilful hand, with true love-guided art,
Had traced the image graven on her heart.
"Art thou all present? Dost thou fail to see
Poor UMÁ's anguish and her love for thee?"
Thus oft in frenzied grief her voice was heard,
Chiding the portrait with reproachful word.
Long thus in vain for ŚIVA's love she strove,
Then turned in sorrow to this holy grove.
Since the sad maid hath sought these forest glades
To hide her grief amid the dreary shades,
The fruit hath ripened on the spreading bough;
But ah! no fruit hath crowned her holy vow.
Her faithful friends alone must ever mourn
To see that beauteous form by penance worn,
But oh! that ŚIVA would some favour deign,
As INDRA pitieth the parching plain!"

The maiden ceased: his secret joy dissembling,
The Bráhman turned to UMÁ pale and trembling:
"And is it thus, or doth the maiden jest?
Is this the darling secret of thy breast?"

Scarce could the maid her choking voice command,
Or clasp her rosary with quivering hand:
"O holy Sage, learned in the Vedas' lore,
'Tis even thus. Great ŚIVA I adore.
Thus would my steadfast heart his love obtain,
For this I gladly bear the toil and pain.

Surely the strong desire, the earnest will,
May win some favour from his mercy still."

"Lady," cried he, "that mighty Lord I know;
Ever his presence bringeth care and woe.
And wouldst thou still a second time prepare
The sorrows of his fearful life to share?
Deluded maid, how shall thy tender hand,
Decked with the nuptial bracelet's jewelled band,
Be clasped in his, when fearful serpents twine
In scaly horror round that arm divine?
How shall thy robe, with gay flamingoes gleaming,
Suit with his coat of hide with blood-drops streaming?
Of old thy pathway led where flowerets sweet
Made pleasant carpets for thy gentle feet.
And e'en thy foes would turn in grief away
To see these vermeil-tinted limbs essay,
Where scattered tresses strew the mournful place,
Their gloomy path amid the tombs to trace.
On Śiva's heart the funeral ashes rest,
Say, gentle lady, shall they stain thy breast,
Where the rich tribute of the Sandal trees
Sheds a pure odour on the amorous breeze?
A royal bride returning in thy state,
The king of elephants should bear thy weight.
How wilt thou brook the mockery and the scorn
When thou on Śiva's bull art meanly borne?

Sad that the crescent moon his crest should be:
And shall that mournful fate be shared by thee?
His crest, the glory of the evening skies,
His bride, the moonlight of our wondering eyes!
Deformed is he, his ancestry unknown;
By vilest garb his poverty is shown.
O fawn-eyed lady, how should ŚIVA gain
That heart for which the glorious strive in vain
No charms hath he to win a maiden's eye:
Cease from thy penance, hush the fruitless sigh!
Unmeet is he thy faithful heart to share,
Child of the Mountain, maid of beauty rare!
Not 'mid the gloomy tombs do sages raise
The holy altar of their prayer and praise."

Impatient UMÁ listened: the quick blood
Rushed to her temples in an angry flood.
Her quivering lip, her darkly-flashing eye
Told that the tempest of her wrath was nigh.
Proudly she spoke: " How couldst thou tell aright
Of one like ŚIVA, perfect, infinite?
'Tis ever thus, the mighty and the just
Are scorned by souls that grovel in the dust.
Their lofty goodness and their motives wise
Shine all in vain before such blinded eyes.

## UMÁ'S REWARD.

Say who is greater, he who strives for power,
Or he who succours in misfortune's hour?
Refuge of worlds, O how should ŚIVA deign
To look on men enslaved to paltry gain?
The spring of wealth himself, he careth naught
For the vile treasures that mankind have sought.
His dwelling-place amid the tombs may be,
Yet Monarch of the three great worlds is he.
What though no love his outward form may claim,
The stout heart trembles at his awful name.
Who can declare the wonders of his might?
The Trident-wielding God, who knows aright?
Whether around him deadly serpents twine,
Or if his jewelled wreaths more brightly shine;
Whether in rough and wrinkled hide arrayed,
Or silken robe, in glittering folds displayed;
If on his brow the crescent moon he bear,
Or if a shrunken skull be withering there;
The funeral ashes touched by him acquire
The glowing lustre of eternal fire;
Falling in golden showers, the heavenly maids
Delight to pour them on their shining braids.
What though no treasures fill his storehouse full,
What though he ride upon his horned bull,
Not e'en may INDRA in his pride withhold
The lowly homage that is his of old,

But turns his raging elephant to meet
His mighty Lord, and bows before his feet,
Right proud to colour them rich rosy red
With the bright flowers that deck his prostrate head.
Thy slanderous tongue proclaims thy evil mind,
Yet in thy speech one word of truth we find.
Unknown thou call'st him : how should mortal man
Count when the days of BRAHMÁ's Lord began ?
But cease these idle words : though all be true,
His failings many and his virtues few,
Still clings my heart to him, its chosen lord,
Nor fails nor falters at thy treacherous word.
Dear maiden, bid yon eager boy depart :
Why should the slanderous tale defile his heart ?
Most guilty who the faithless speech begins,
But he who stays to listen also sins."

 She turned away : with wrath her bosom swelling,
Its vest of bark in angry pride repelling :
But sudden, lo, before her wondering eyes
In altered form she sees the sage arise ;
'Tis ŚIVA's self before the astonished maid,
In all his gentlest majesty displayed.
She saw, she trembled, like a river's course,
Checked for a moment in its onward force,
By some huge rock amid the torrent hurled
Where erst the foaming waters madly curled.

One foot uplifted, shall she turn away?
Unmoved the other, shall the maiden stay?
The silver moon on ŚIVA'S forehead shone,
While softly spake the God in gracious tone:
" O gentle maiden, wise and true of soul,
Lo, now I bend beneath thy sweet control.
Won by thy penance, and thy holy vows,
Thy willing slave ŚIVA before thee bows."

He spake, and rushing through her languid frame,
At his dear words returning vigour came.
She knew but this, that all her cares were o'er,
Her sorrows ended, she should weep no more!

## CANTO SIXTH.

# Canto Sixth.

―――o―――

## UMÁ'S ESPOUSALS.

Now gentle UMÁ bade a damsel bear
To ŚIVA, Soul of All, her maiden prayer:
" Wait the high sanction of HIMÁLAYA's will,
And ask his daughter from the royal hill."
Then ere the God, her own dear Lord, replied,
In blushing loveliness she sought his side.
Thus the young mango hails the approaching spring
By its own tuneful bird's sweet welcoming.

In UMÁ's ear he softly whispered, yea,
Then scarce could tear him from her arms away.
Swift with a thought he summoned from above
The Seven bright Saints to bear his tale of love.
They came, and She, the Heavenly Dame, was there,
Lighting with glories all the radiant air;
Just freshly bathed in sacred GANGÁ's tide,
Gemmed with the dancing flowers that deck her side,

And richly scented with the nectarous rill
That heavenly elephants from their brows distil.
Fair strings of pearl their radiant fingers hold,
Clothed are their limbs in hermit-coats of gold;
Their rosaries, large gems of countless price,
Shone like the fruit that glows in Paradise,
As though the glorious trees that blossom there
Had sought the forest for a life of prayer.
With all his thousand beams the God of Day,
Urging his coursers down the sloping way,
His banner furled at the approach of night,
Looks up in reverence on those lords of light.
Ancient creators: thus the wise, who know,
Gave them a name in ages long ago:
With BRAHMÁ joining in creation's plan,
And perfecting the work His will began;
Still firm in penance, though the hermit-vow
Bears a ripe harvest for the sages now.
Brightest in glory 'mid that glorious band
See the fair Queen, the Heavenly Lady, stand.
Fixing her loving eyes upon her spouse,
She seemed sent forth to crown the sage's vows
With sweet immortal joy, the dearest prize
Strong prayer could merit from the envious skies.
With equal honour on the Queen and all
Did the kind glance of ŚIVA's welcome fall.

No partial favour by the good is shown:
They count not station, but the deed alone.
So fair she shone upon his raptured view,
He longed for wedlock's heavenly pleasures too.
What hath such power to lead the soul above
By virtue's pleasant path as wedded love!
Scarce had the holy motive lent its aid
To knit great ŚIVA to the Mountain-Maid,
When KÁMA's spirit that had swooned in fear
Breathed once again and deemed forgiveness near.

 The ancient Sages reverently adored
The world's great Father and its Sovran Lord,
And while a soft ecstatic thrilling ran
O'er their celestial frames, they thus began:
 "Glorious the fruit our holy studies bear,
Our constant penance, sacrifice and prayer.
For that high place within thy thoughts we gain
Which fancy strives to reach, but longs in vain.
How blest is he, the glory of the wise,
Deep in whose thoughtful breast thy Godhead lies!
But who may tell his joy who rests enshrined,
O BRAHMÁ's great Creator, in thy mind!
We dwell on high above the cold moon's ray;
Beneath our mansion glows the God of Day,
But now thy favour lends us brighter beams,
Blest with thy love our star unchanging gleams.

How should we tell what soul-entrancing bliss
Enthrals our spirit at an hour like this?
Great Lord of All, thou Soul of Life indwelling,
We crave one word thy wondrous nature telling.
Though to our eyes thy outward form be shown,
How can we know thee as thou shouldst be known?
In this thy present shape, we pray thee, say
Dost thou create? dost thou preserve or slay?
But speak thy wish; called from our starry rest
We wait, O Śiva, for our Lord's behest."

Then answered thus the Lord of glory, while
Flashed from his dazzling teeth so white a smile,
The moon that crowned him poured a larger stream
Of living splendour from that pearly gleam:
" Ye know, great Sages of a race divine,
No selfish want e'er prompts a deed of mine.
Do not the forms—eight varied forms—I wear,
The truth of this to all the world declare?
Now, as that thirsty bird that drinks the rain
Prays the kind clouds of heaven to soothe its pain,
So the Gods pray me, trembling 'neath their foe,
To send a child of mine and end their woe.
I seek the Mountain-Maiden as my bride:
Our hero son shall tame the demon's pride.

Thus the priest bids the holy fire arise,
Struck from the wood to aid the sacrifice.
Go, ask HIMÁLAYA for the lovely maid:
Blest are those bridals which the holy aid.
So shall more glorious honours gild my name,
And win the father yet a prouder fame.
Nor, O ye heavenly Sages, need I teach
What for the maiden's hand shall be your speech,
For still the wise in worthiest honour hold
The rules and precepts ye ordained of old.
This Lady too shall aid your mission there:
Best for such task a skilful matron's care.
And now, my heralds, to your task away,
Where proud HIMÁLAYA holds his royal sway;
Then meet me where this mighty torrent raves
Down the steep channel with its headlong waves."

Thus while that holiest One his love confessed,
The hermits listened: from each saintly breast
Fled the false shame that yet had lingered there,
And love and wedlock showed divinely fair.

On through the heaven, o'er tracts of swordlike blue,
Towards the gay city, swift as thought, they flew,
Bright with high domes and palaces most fair,
As if proud ALAKÁ were planted there,

Or PARADISE poured forth, in showers that bless,
The rich o'erflowings of its loveliness.
Round lofty towers adorned with gems and gold
Her guardian stream the holy GANGÁ rolled.
On every side, the rampart's glowing crown,
Bright wreaths of fragrant flowers hung waving down,—
Flowers that might tempt the maids of heavenly birth
To linger fondly o'er that pride of earth.
Its noble elephants, unmoved by fear,
The distant roaring of the lions hear.
In beauty peerless, and unmatched in speed,
Its thousand coursers of celestial breed.
Through the broad streets bright sylphs and minstrels rove:
Its dames are Goddesses of stream and grove.

 Hark! the drum echoes louder and more loud
From glittering halls whose spires are wrapt in cloud.
It were the thunder, but that voice of fear
Falls not in measured time upon the ear.
'Tis balmy cool, for many a heavenly tree,
With quivering leaves and branches waving free,
Sheds a delightful freshness through the air,—
Fans which no toil of man has stationed there.
The crystal chambers where they feast at night
Flash back the beamings of the starry light.
So brightly pure that silver gleam is shed,
Playing so fondly round each beauteous head,

That all seem gifted from those lights above
With richest tokens of superior love.
How blest its maidens ! cloudless is their day,
And radiant herbs illume their nightly way.
No term of days, but endless youth they know ;
No Death save him who bears the Flowery Bow :
Their direst swoon, their only frenzy this—
The trance of love, the ecstasy of bliss !
Ne'er can their lovers for one hour withstand
The frown, the quivering lip, the scornful hand ;
But seek forgiveness of the angry fair,
And woo her smile with many an earnest prayer.
Around, wide gardens spread their pleasant bowers,
Where the bright Champac opes her fragrant
    flowers :
Dear shades, beloved by the sylphs that roam
In dewy evening from their mountain home.

Ah ! why should mortals fondly strive to gain
Heaven and its joys by ceaseless toil and pain ?
E'en the Saints envied as their steps drew near,
And owned a brighter heaven was opened here.
They lighted down ; braided was each long tress,
Bright as the pictured flame, as motionless.
HIMÁLAYA'S palace-warders in amaze
On the Seven Sages turned their eager gaze,—

A noble company of celestial race
Where each in order of his years had place,—
Glorious, as when the sun, his head inclining,
Sees his own image 'mid the waters shining.
 To greet them with a gift HIMÁLAYA sped,
Earth to her centre shaking at his tread.
By his dark lips with mountain metals dyed,
His arms like pines that clothe his lofty side:
By his proud stature, by his stony breast,
Lord of the Snowy Hills he stood confest.
On to his Council-hall he led the way,
Nor failed due honour to the Saints to pay.
On couch of reed the Monarch bade them rest,
And thus with uplift hands those Heavenly Lords
  addressed:
"Like soft rain falling from a cloudless sky,
Or fruit, when bloom has failed to glad the eye,
So are ye welcome, Sages; thus I feel
Ecstatic thrilling o'er my spirit steal,
Changed, like dull senseless iron to burning gold,
Or some rapt creature, when the heavens unfold
To eyes yet dim with tears of earthly care,
The rest, the pleasures, and the glory there.
Long pilgrim bands from this auspicious day
To my pure hill shall bend their constant way.
Famed shall it be o'er all the lands around,
For where the good have been is holy ground.

Now am I doubly pure, for GANGÁ's tide
Falls on my head from heaven and laves my side.
Henceforth I boast a second stream as sweet,
The water, Sages, that has touched your feet.
Twice by your favour is HIMÁLAYA blest,—
This towery mountain that your feet have prest,
And this my moving form is happier still
To wait your bidding, to perform your will.
These mighty limbs that fill the heaven's expanse
Sink down, o'erpowered, in a blissful trance.
So bright your presence, at the glorious sight
My brooding shades of darkness turn to light.
The gloom that haunts my mountain caverns flies,
And cloudy passion in the spirit dies.
O say, if here your arrowy course ye sped
To throw fresh glory round my towering head.
Surely your wish, ye Mighty Ones, can crave
No aid, no service from your willing slave.
Yet deem me worthy of some high behest:
The lord commandeth, and the slave is blest.
Declare your pleasure, then, bright heavenly band:
We crave no guerdon but your sole command.
Yours are we all, HIMÁLAYA and his bride,
And this dear maiden child our hope and pride."

Not once he spake: his cavern mouths around
In hollow echoings gave again the sound.

Of all who speak beyond compare the best,
ANGIRAS answered at the Saints' request:
 "This power hast thou, great King, and mightier far,
Thy mind is lofty as thy summits are.
Sages say truly, VISHNU is thy name:
His spirit breatheth in thy mountain frame.
Within the caverns of thy boundless breast
All things that move and all that move not rest.
How on his head so soft, so delicate,
Could the great Snake uphold the huge earth's weight,
Did not thy roots, far-reaching down to hell,
Bear up the burden and assist him well?
Thy streams of praise, thy pure rills' ceaseless flow
Make glad the nations wheresoe'er they go,
Till, shedding purity on every side,
They sink at length in boundless Ocean's tide.
Blest is fair GANGÁ, for her heavenly stream
Flows from the feet of him that sits supreme;
And blest once more, O mighty Hill, is she
That her bright waters spring anew from thee.
Vast grew his body when the avenging God
In three huge strides o'er all creation trod.
Above, below, his form increased, but thou
Wast ever glorious and as vast as now.
By thee is famed SUMERU forced to hide
His flashing rays and pinnacles of pride,

For thou hast won thy station in the skies
'Mid the great Gods who claim the sacrifice.
Firm and unmoved remains thy lofty hill,
Yet thou canst bow before the holy still.
Now—for the glorious work will fall on thee,—
Hear thou the cause of this our embassy.
We also, Mountain Monarch, since we bear
To thee the message, in the labour share.
The Highest, Mightiest, Noblest One, adored
By the proud title of our Sovran Lord:
The crescent moon upon his brow bears he,
And wields the wondrous powers of Deity.
He in this earth and varied forms displayed,
Bound each to other by exchange of aid,
Guides the great world and all the things that are,
As flying coursers whirl the glittering car.
Him good men seek with holy thought and prayer,
Who fills their breast and makes his dwelling there.
When saints, we read, his lofty sphere attain,
They ne'er may fall to this base earth again:
His messengers, great King, we crave the hand
Of thy fair daughter at the God's command.
At such blest union, as of TRUTH and VOICE,
A father's heart should grieve not, but rejoice.
Her Lord is Father of the world, and she
Of all that liveth shall the mother be.

Gods that adore him with the Neck of Blue
In homage bent shall hail the Lady too,
And give a glory to her feet with gems
That sparkle in their priceless diadems.
Hear what a roll shall blazon forth thy line,—
Maid, Father, Suitor, Messengers divine!
Give him the chosen lady, and aspire
To call thy son the Universe's Sire,
Who laudeth none, but all mankind shall raise
To Him through endless time the songs of praise."

Thus while he spake the lady bent her head
To hide her cheek, now blushing rosy red,
And numbered o'er with seeming care the while
Her lotus' petals in sweet maiden guile.
With pride and joy HIMÁLAYA's heart beat high,
Yet ere he spake he looked to MENÁ's eye:
Full well he knew a mother's gentle care
Learns her child's heart and love's deep secret
        there,
And this the hour, he felt, when fathers seek
Her eye for answer or her changing cheek.
His eager look HIMÁLAYA scarce had bent
When MENÁ's eye beamed back her glad assent.
O gentle wives! your fondest wish is still
To have with him you love one heart, one will.

He threw his arms around the blushing maid
In queenly garment and in gems arrayed,
Awhile was silent, then in rapture cried,
"Come, O my daughter! Come, thou destined bride
Of Śiva, Lord of All: this glorious band
Of Saints have sought thee at the God's command;
And I thy sire this happy day obtain
The best reward a father's wish would gain."
Then to the Saints he cried: " Pure Hermits, see
The spouse of Śiva greets your company."
They looked in rapture on the maid, and poured
Their fullest blessing on her heavenly lord.
So low she bowed, the gems that decked her hair
And sparkled in her ear fell loosened there;
Then with sweet modesty and joy opprest
She hid her blushes on the Lady's breast,
Who cheered the mother weeping for her child,
Her own dear Umá, till again she smiled:
Such bliss and glory should be hers above,
Yea, mighty Śiva's undivided love.

They named the fourth for Umá's nuptial day;
Then sped the Sages on their homeward way;
And thanked by Śiva with a gracious eye
Sought their bright rest amid the stars on high.

Through all those weary days the lover sighed
To wind his fond arms round his gentle bride.
Oh, if the Lord of Heaven could find no rest,
Think, think how Love, strong Love, can tear a mortal's
    breast!

## CANTO SEVENTH.

# Canto Seventh.

## UMÁ'S BRIDAL.

In light and glory dawned the expected day
Blest with a kindly star's auspicious ray,
When gaily gathered at HIMÁLAYA's call
His kinsmen to the solemn festival.
Through the broad city every dame's awake
To grace the bridal for her monarch's sake;
So great their love for him, this single care
Makes one vast household of the thousands there.
Heaven is not brighter than the royal street
Where flowers lie scattered 'neath the nobles' feet,
And banners waving to the breeze unfold
Their silken broidery over gates of gold.
And she, their child, upon her bridal day
Bears her dear parents' every thought away.
So, when from distant shores a friend returns,
With deeper love each inmost spirit burns.

So, when grim Death restores his prey again
Joy brighter shines from memory of pain.
Each noble matron of HIMÁLAYA'S race
Folds his dear UMÁ in a long embrace,
Pours blessings on her head, and prays her take
Some priceless jewel for her friendship's sake.
With sweetest influence a star of power
Had joined the spotted moon: at that blest hour
To deck fair UMÁ many a noble dame
And many a gentle maid assiduous came.
And well she graced their toil, more brightly fair
With feathery grass and wild flowers in her hair.
A silken robe flowed free below her waist;
Her sumptuous head a glittering arrow graced.
So shines the young unclouded moon at last,
Greeting the sun, its darksome season past.
Sweet-scented Lodhra dust and Sandal dyed
The delicate beauties of the fair young bride,
Veiled with a soft light robe. Her tiring-girls
Then led her to a chamber decked with pearls
And paved with sapphires, where the lulling sound
Of choicest music breathed divinely round.
There o'er the lady's limbs they poured by turns
Streams of pure water from their golden urns.
Fresh from the cooling bath the lovely maid
In fairest white her tender form arrayed.

So opes the Kása all her shining flowers
Lured from their buds by softly falling showers.
Then to a court with canopies o'erhead
A crowd of noble dames the maiden led—
A court for solemn rites, where gems and gold
Adorn the pillars that the roof uphold.
There on a couch they set her with her face
Turned toward the east. So lovely then the grace
Of that dear maid, so ravishing her smile,
E'en her attendants turned to gaze awhile;
For though the brightest gems around her lay,
Her brighter beauty stole their eyes away.
Through her long tresses one a chaplet wound,
And one with fragrant grass her temples crowned,
While o'er her head sweet clouds of incense rolled
To try and perfume every shining fold.
Bright dyes of saffron and the scented wood
Adorned her beauty, till the maiden stood
Fairer than GANGÁ when the Love-birds play
O'er sandy islets in her silvery bay.
To what rare beauty shall her maids compare
Her clear brow shaded by her glossy hair?
Less dazzling pure the lovely lotus shines
Flecked by the thronging bees in dusky lines.
Less bright the moon, when a dark band of cloud
Enhances beauties which it cannot shroud.

Behind her ear a head of barley drew
The eye to gaze upon its golden hue.
But then her cheek, with glowing saffron dyed,
To richer beauty called the glance aside.
Though from those lips, where Beauty's guerdon
      lay,
The vermeil tints were newly washed away,
Yet o'er them, as she smiled, a ray was thrown
Of quivering brightness that was all their own.

"Lay this dear foot upon thy lover's head
Crowned with the moon," the laughing maiden said,
Who dyed her lady's feet—no word spake she,
But beat her with her wreath in playful glee.
Then tiring-women took the jetty dye
To guard, not deck, the beauty of her eye,
Whose languid half-shut glances might compare
With lotus leaves just opening to the air;
And as fresh gems adorned her neck and arms,
So quickly changing grew the maiden's charms,
Like some fair plant where bud succeeding bud
Unfolds new beauty; or a silver flood
Where gay birds follow quickly; or like night,
When crowding stars come forth in all their light.
Oft as the mirror would her glance beguile
She longed to meet her Lord's approving smile.

Her tasteful skill the timid maid essays
To win one smile of love, one word of praise.

   The happy mother took the golden dye
And raised to hers young UMÁ's beaming eye.
Then swelled her bosom with maternal pride
As thus she decked her darling for a bride.
Oh, she had longed to trace on that fair brow
The nuptial line, yet scarce could mark it now.
   On UMÁ's rounded arm the woollen band
Was fixt securely by the nurse's hand.
Blind with the tears that filled her swimming eye,
In vain the mother strove that band to tie.
Spotless as curling foam-flakes stood she there,
As yielding soft, as graceful and as fair:
Or like the glory of an autumn night
Robed by the full moon in a veil of light.
   Then at her mother's hest, the maid adored
The spirit of each high ancestral lord,
Nor failed she next the noble dames to greet,
And give due honour to their reverend feet.
They raised the maiden as she bowed her head:
"Thine be the fulness of his love!" they said.
Half of his being, blessing high as this
Can add no rapture to her perfect bliss.
   Well-pleased HIMÁLAYA viewed the pomp and pride
Meet for his daughter, meet for ŚIVA's bride;

Then sought the hall with all his friends to wait
The bridegroom's coming with a monarch's state.

 Meanwhile by heavenly matrons' care displayed
Upon KUVERA's lofty mount were laid
The ornaments of SIVA, which of yore
At his first nuptials the bridegroom wore.
He laid his hand upon the dress, but how
Shall robes so sad, so holy, grace him now?
His own dire vesture took a shape as fair
As gentle bridegroom's heart could wish to wear.
The withering skull that glazed the eye with
   dread,
Shone a bright coronal to grace his head.
That elephant's hide the God had worn of old
Was now a silken robe inwrought with gold.
Ere this his body was with dust besprent:
With unguent now it shed delightful scent;
And that mid-eye which glittering like a star
Shot the wild terror of its glance afar—
So softly now its golden radiance beamed—
A mark of glory on his forehead seemed.
His twining serpents, destined still to be
The pride and honour of the deity,
Changed but their bodies: in each sparkling crest
The blazing gems still shone their loveliest.

What need of jewels on the brow of Him
Who wears the crescent moon? No spot may dim
Its youthful beauty, e'en in light of day
Shedding the glory of its quenchless ray.
Well-pleased the God in all his pride arrayed
Saw his bright image mirrored in the blade
Of the huge sword they brought; then calmly
    leant
On NANDI's arm, and toward his bull he went,
Whose broad back covered with a tiger's hide
Was steep to climb as Mount KAILÁSA's side.
Yet the dread monster humbly shrank for fear,
And bowed in reverence as his Lord drew near.
The matrons followed him, a saintly throng,
Their ear-rings waving as they dashed along:
Sweet faces, with such glories round them shed
As made the air one lovely lotus bed.
On flew those bright ones: KÁLI came behind,
The skulls that decked her rattling in the wind:
Like the dark rack that scuds across the sky,
With herald lightning and the crane's shrill cry.

Hark! from the glorious bands that lead the way,
Harp, drum, and pipe, and shrilling trumpet's bray,
Burst through the sky upon the startled ear
And tell the Gods the hour of worship's near.

They came; the Sun presents a silken shade
Which heaven's own artist for the God had made,
Gilding his brows, as though bright Gangá rolled
Adown his holy head her waves of gold.
She in her Goddess-shape divinely fair,
And Yamuná, sweet River-Nymph, were there,
Fanning their Lord, that fancy still might deem
Swans waved their pinions round each Lady of the Stream.
E'en Brahmá came, Creator, Lord of Might,
And Vishṇu glowing from the realms of light.
"Ride on," they cried, "thine, thine for ever be
The strength, the glory, and the victory."
To swell his triumph that high blessing came
Like holy oil upon the rising flame.
In those Three Persons the one God was shown,
Each first in place, each last,—not one alone;
Of Śiva, Vishṇu, Brahmá, each may be
First, second, third, among the Blessed Three.
By Indra led, each world-upholding Lord
With folded hands the mighty God adored.
In humble robes arrayed, the pomp and pride
Of glorious deity they laid aside.
They signed to Nandi, and the favourite's hand
Guided his eye upon the suppliant band.
He spake to Vishṇu, and on Indra smiled,
To Brahmá bowed—the lotus' mystic child.

On all the hosts of heaven his friendly eye
Beamed duly welcome as they crowded nigh.
The Seven Great Saints their blessings o'er him shed,
And thus in answer, with a smile, he said:
"Hail, mighty Sages! hail, ye Sons of Light!
My chosen priests to celebrate this rite."

 Now in sweet tones the heavenly minstrels tell
His praise, beneath whose might TRIPURA fell.
He moves to go: from his moon-crest a ray
Sheds quenchless light on his triumphant way.
On through the air his swift bull bore him well,
Decked with the gold of many a tinkling bell;
Tossing from time to time his head on high,
Enwreathed with clouds as he flew racing by,
As though in furious charge he had uptorn
A bank of clay upon his mighty horn.

 Swiftly they came where in its beauty lay
The city subject to HIMÁLAYA's sway.
No foeman's foot had ever trod those halls,
No foreign bands encamped around the walls.
Then ŚIVA's glances fixed their eager hold
On that fair city as with threads of gold.
The God whose neck still gleams with cloudy blue
Burst on the wondering people's upturned view,
And on the earth descended, from the path
His shafts once dinted in avenging wrath.

Forth from the gates a noble army poured
To do meet honour to the mighty Lord.
With all his friends on elephants of state
The King of Mountains passed the city gate,
So gaily decked, the princes all were seen
Like moving hills inwrapt in bowery green.
As the full rushing of two streams that pour
Beneath one bridge with loud tumultuous roar,
So through the city's open gate streamed in
Mountains and Gods with tumult and with din.
So glorious was the sight, wonder and shame,
When ŚIVA bowed him, o'er the Monarch came;
He knew not he had bent his lofty crest
In reverent greeting to his heavenly guest.
HIMÁLAYA, joying in the festive day,
Before the immortal bridegroom led the way
Where heaps of gay flowers burying half the feet
Lay breathing odours through the crowded street.

   Careless of all beside, each lady's eye
Must gaze on ŚIVA as the troop sweeps by.
One dark-eyed beauty will not stay to bind
Her long black tresses, floating unconfined
Save by her little hand; her flowery crown
Hanging neglected and unfastened down.
One from her maiden tore her foot away
On which the dye, all wet and streaming, lay,

And o'er the chamber rushing in her haste,
Where'er she stepped, a crimson footprint traced.
Another at the window takes her stand;
One eye is dyed,—the pencil in her hand.
Here runs an eager maid, and running, holds
Loose and ungirt her flowing mantle's folds,
Whilst, as she strives to close the parting vest,
Its brightness gives new beauty to her breast.
Oh! what a sight! the crowded windows there
With eager faces excellently fair,
Like sweetest lilies, for their dark eyes fling
Quick glances quivering like the wild bee's wing.

   Onward in peerless glory ŚIVA passed;
Gay banners o'er his way their shadows cast,
Each palace dome, each pinnacle and height
Catching new lustre from his crest of light.
On swept the pageant: on the God alone
The eager glances of the dames were thrown;
On his bright form they fed the rapturous gaze,
And only turned to marvel and to praise:
" Oh, well and wisely, such a lord to gain
The Mountain-Maid endured the toil and pain.
To be his slave were joy; but Oh, how blest
The wife—the loved one—lying on his breast!
Surely in vain, had not the Lord of Life
Matched this fond bridegroom and this loving wife,

Had been his wish to give the worlds a mould
Of perfect beauty!  Falsely have they told
How the young flower-armed God was burnt by fire
At the red flash of Śiva's vengeful ire.
No: jealous Love a fairer form confessed,
And cast away his own, no more the loveliest.
How glorious is the Mountain King, how proud
Earth's stately pillar, girt about with cloud!
Now will he lift his lofty head more high,
Knit close to Śiva by this holy tie."

Such words of praise from many a bright-eyed
       dame
On Śiva's ear with soothing witchery came.
Through the broad streets 'mid loud acclaim he rode,
And reached the palace where the King abode.
There he descended from his monster's side,
As the sun leaves a cloud at eventide.
Leaning on Vishṇu's arm he passed the door
Where mighty Brahmá entered in before.
Next Indra came, and all the host of heaven,
The noble Saints and those great Sages seven.
Then led they Śiva to a royal seat;
Fair gifts they brought, for such a bridegroom meet:
With all due rites, the honey and the milk,
Rich gems were offered and two robes of silk.

   At length by skilful chamberlains arrayed
They led the lover to the royal maid.
Thus the fond Moon disturbs the tranquil rest
Of Ocean glittering with his foamy crest,
And leads him on, his proud waves swelling o'er,
To leap with kisses on the clasping shore.
He gazed on UMÁ. From his lotus eyes
Flashed out the rapture of his proud surprise.
Then calm the current of his spirit lay
Like the world basking in an autumn day.

   They met; and true love's momentary shame
O'er the blest bridegroom and his darling came.
Eye looked to eye, but, quivering as they met,
Scarce dared to trust the rapturous gazing yet.

   In the God's hand the priest has duly laid
The radiant fingers of the Mountain-Maid,
Bright, as if LOVE with his dear sprays of red
Had sought that refuge in his hour of dread.
From hand to hand the soft infection stole,
Till each confessed it in the inmost soul.
Fire filled his veins, with joy she trembled; such
The magic influence of that thrilling touch.

   How grows their beauty, when two lovers stand
Eye fixt on eye, hand fondly linkt in hand!

Then how, unblamed, may mortal minstrel dare
To paint in words the beauty of that pair!
   Around the fire in solemn rite they trod,
The lovely lady and the glorious God;
Like day and starry midnight when they meet
In the broad plains at lofty MERU's feet.
Thrice at the bidding of the priest they came
With swimming eyes around the holy flame.
Then at his word the bride in order due
Into the blazing fire the parched grain threw,
And toward her face the scented smoke she drew,
Which softly wreathing o'er her fair cheek hung,
And round her ears in flower-like beauty clung.
As o'er the incense the sweet lady stooped,
The ear of barley from her tresses drooped,
And rested on her cheek, beneath the eye
Still brightly beaming with the jetty dye.

   "This flame be witness of your wedded life:
Be just, thou husband, and be true, thou wife!"
Such was the priestly blessing on the bride.
Eager she listened, as the earth when dried
By parching summer suns drinks deeply in
The first soft droppings when the rains begin.

   "Look, gentle UMÁ," cried her Lord, "afar
Seest thou the brightness of yon polar star?

Like that unchanging ray thy faith must shine."
Sobbing, she whispered, " Yes, for ever thine."


The rite is o'er. Her joyful parents now
At Brahmá's feet in duteous reverence bow.
Then to fair Umá spake the gracious Power
Who sits enthroned upon the lotus flower:
" O beautiful lady, happy shalt thou be,
And hero children shall be born of thee;"
Then looked in silence: vain the hope to bless
The bridegroom, Śiva, with more happiness.


Then from the altar, as prescribed of old,
They turned, and rested upon seats of gold;
And, as the holy books for men ordain,
Were sprinkled duly with the moistened grain.
High o'er their heads sweet Beauty's Queen displayed
Upon a stem of reed a cool green shade,
While the young lotus-leaves of which 'twas made
Seemed, as they glistened to the wondering view,
All richly pearled with drops of beady dew.
In twofold language on each glorious head
The Queen of Speech her richest blessings shed;
In strong, pure, godlike utterance for his ear,
To her in liquid tones, soft, beautifully clear.

Now for awhile they gaze where maids divine
In graceful play the expressive dance entwine;
Whose eloquent motions, with an actor's art,
Show to the life the passions of the heart.

The rite was ended; then the heavenly band
Prayed ŚIVA, raising high the suppliant hand:
" Now, for the dear sake of thy lovely bride,
Have pity on the gentle God," they cried,
" Whose tender body thy fierce wrath has slain:
Give all his honour, all his might again."
Well pleased, he smiled, and gracious answer gave:
ŚIVA himself now yields him KÁMA's slave.
When duly given, the great will ne'er despise
The gentle pleading of the good and wise.

Now have they left the wedded pair alone;
And ŚIVA takes her hand within his own
To lead his darling to the bridal bower,
Decked with bright gold and all her sumptuous dower.
She blushes sweetly as her maidens there
Look with arch smiles and glances on the pair;
And for one moment, while the damsels stay,
From him she loves turns her dear face away.

# NOTES.

## CANTO FIRST.

THE Hindú Deity of War, the leader of the celestial armies, is known by the names Kártikeya and Skanda. He is represented with six faces and corresponding arms, and is mounted upon a peacock.

*Himálaya.*] Mansion of Snow; from *hima*, snow, and *álaya*, mansion. The accent is on the *second* syllable.

*Prithu.*] It is said that in the reign of this fabulous monarch, gods, saints, demons, and other supernatural beings, drained or *milked* from the earth various treasures, appointing severally one of their own class as the recipient, or *Calf*, to use the word of the legend. Himálaya was thus highly favoured by the sacred Mount Meru, and the other hills. The story is found in the sixth chapter of the *Harivansa*, which forms a supplement to the *Mahabhárat*.

*Still the fair pearls, &c.*] It was the belief of the Hindús that elephants wore these precious jewels in their heads.

*Till heavenly minstrels, &c.*] A class of demi-gods, the songsters of the Hindú Paradise, or Indra's heaven.

*There magic herbs, &c.*] Frequent allusion is made by Kálidás and other Sanskrit poets to a phosphoric light emitted by plants at night.

*E'en the wild kine, &c.*] The *Chouri*, or long brush, used to whisk off insects and flies, was with the Hindús what the sceptre is with us. It was usually made of the tail-hairs of the *Yak*, or *Bos Grunniens*. Thus the poet represents these animals as doing honour to the Monarch of Mountains with these emblems of sovereignty.

*That the bright Seven.*] The Hindús call the constellation *Ursa Major* the seven Rishis, or Saints. They will appear as actors in the course of the poem.

*And once when Indra's might.*] We learn from the *Rámáyana* that the mountains were originally furnished with wings, and that they flew through the air with the speed of the wind. For fear lest they should suddenly fall in their flight, Indra, King of the Gods, struck off their pinions with his thunderbolt; but Maináka was preserved from a similar fate by the friendship of Ocean, to whom he fled for refuge.

*Born once again, &c.*] The reader will remember the Hindú belief in the Transmigration of Souls. The story alluded to by the poet is this:—"*Daksha* was the son of *Brahmá* and father of *Satí*, whom, at the recommendation of the *Rishis*, or Sages, he espoused to *Śiva*, but he was never wholly reconciled to the uncouth figure and practices of his son-in-law. Having undertaken to celebrate a solemn sacrifice, he invited all the Gods except *Śiva*, which so incensed *Satí*, that she threw herself into the sacrificial fire."—(Wilson, Specimens of Hindú Theatre, Vol. II. p. 263.) The name of *Satí*, meaning good, true, chaste woman, is the modern *Suttee*, as it is corruptly written.

*As the blue offspring of the Turquois Hills.*] These hills are placed in Ceylon. The precious stone grows, it is said, at the sound of thunder in the rainy season.

*At her stern penance.*] This is described in the fifth canto. The meaning of the name Umá is "Oh, do not."

*The Gods' bright river.*] The celestial Ganges, which falls from heaven upon Himálaya's head, and continues its course on earth.

*Young Káma's arrow.*] Káma, the Hindú Cupid, is armed with a bow, the arrows of which are made of flowers.

*And brighter than Aśoka's rich leaves.*] Nothing, we are told, can exceed the beauty of this tree when in full bloom. It is, of course, a general favourite with the poets of India.

*The strings of pearl.*]
> " Then, too, the pearl from out its shell
> Unsightly, in the sunless sea
> (As 'twere a spirit, forced to dwell
> In form unlovely) *was set free,*
> And round the neck of woman threw
> *A light it lent and borrowed too.*"
>
> MOORE—*Loves of the Angels.*

Moore is frequently the best interpreter, unconsciously, of an Indian poet's thought. It is worth remarking, that the Sanskrit word *muktá*, pearl (literally *freed*), signifies also the *spirit* released from mundane existence, and re-integrated with its divine original.

*The sweetest note that e'er the Köil poured.*] The *Kokila*, or *Köil*, the black or Indian cuckoo, is the bulbul or nightingale of Hindústan. It is also the herald of spring, like its European namesake, and the female bird is the especial messenger of Love.

*When holy Nárad.*] A divine sage, son of Brahmá.

*The holy bull.*] The animal on which the God Śiva rides, as Indra on the elephant.

*Who takes eight various forms.*] Śiva is called Wearer of the Eight Forms, as being identical with the Five Elements, Mind, Individuality, and Crude Matter.

*Where the pale moon on Śiva's forehead.*] Śiva's crest is the new moon, which is sometimes described as forming a third eye in his forehead. We shall find frequent allusions to this in the course of the poem.

## CANTO SECOND.

*While impious Tárak.*] A demon who, by a long course of austerities, had acquired power even over the Gods. This Hindú notion is familiar to most of us from Southey's " Curse of Keháma."

*Whose face turns every way.*] Brahmá is represented with four faces, one towards each point of the compass.

*The mystic Three.*] "The triad of qualities," a philosophical term familiar to all the systems of Hindú speculation. They are thus explained in the *Tattwa Samása,* a text-book of the Sánkhya school:—"Now it is asked, What is the 'triad of qualities'? It is replied, The triad of qualities consists of 'Goodness,' 'Foulness,' and 'Darkness.' By the 'triad of qualities' is meant the 'three qualities.' Goodness is endlessly diversified, accordingly as it is exemplified in calmness, lightness, complacency, attainment of wishes, kindliness, contentment, patience, joy, and the like; summarily, it consists of happiness. 'Foulness' is endlessly diversified, accordingly as it is exemplified in grief, distress, separation, excitement, anxiety, fault-finding, and the like; summarily, it consists of pain. 'Darkness' is endlessly diversified, accordingly as it is exemplified in envelopment, ignorance, disgust, abjectness, heaviness, sloth, drowsiness, intoxication, and the like; summarily, it consists of delusion."

*Thou, when a longing, &c.*] "Having divided his own substance, the mighty power became half male, half female, or *nature active and passive.*"—*Manu,* Ch. I.

So also in the old Orphic hymn it is said,

Ζεὺς ἄρσην γένετο, Ζεὺς ἄμβροτος ἔπλετο νύμφη.
"Zeus was a male; Zeus was a deathless damsel."

*The sacred hymns.*] Contained in the Vedas, or Holy Scriptures of the Hindús.

*The word of praise.*] The mystic syllable OM, prefacing all the prayers and most of the writings of the Hindús. It implies the Indian triad, and expresses the Three in One.

*They hail thee, Nature.*] The object of Nature's activity, according to the Sánkhya system, is "the final liberation of individual soul." "The incompetency of nature, an irrational principle, to institute a course of action for a definite purpose, and the unfitness of rational soul to regulate the acts of an agent whose character it imperfectly apprehends, constitute a principal argument with the theistical Sánkhyas for the necessity of a Providence, to whom the ends of existence are known, and by whom Nature is guided......The atheistical Sánkhyas, on the other hand, contend that there is no occasion for a guiding Providence, but that the activity of nature, for the purpose of accomplishing soul's object, is an intuitive necessity, as illustrated in the following passage:— As it is a function of milk, an unintelligent (substance), to nourish the calf, so it is the office of the chief principle (nature) to liberate the soul."—Prof. Wilson's *Sánkhya Káriká*.

*Hail Thee the stranger Spirit*, &c.] "Soul is witness, solitary, bystander, spectator, passive."—*Sánkh. Kár.* verse xix.

*See, Varun's noose.*] The God of Water.

*Weak is Kuvera's hand.*] The God of Wealth.

*Yama's sceptre.*] The God and Judge of the Dead.

*The Lords of Light.*] The Ádityas, twelve in number, are forms of the sun, and appear to represent him as distinct in each month of the year.

*The Rudras.*] A class of demi-gods, eleven in number, said to be inferior manifestations of Śiva, who also bears this name.

*E'en as on earth*, &c.] Thus the commandment,—Thou shalt not kill, is abrogated by the injunction to kill animals for sacrifice.

*The heavenly Teacher.*] Vrihaspati, the son of Angiras.

*His own dear flower.*] The lotus, on which Brahmá is represented reclining.

*Their flashing jewels.*] According to the Hindú belief, serpents wear precious jewels in their heads.

*Chakra.*] A discus, or quoit, the weapon of Vishṇu.

*As water bears to me.*] "HE, having willed to produce various beings from his own divine substance, first with a thought created the waters, and placed in them a productive seed."—*Manu*, Ch. I.

*Mournful braids.*] As a sign of mourning, especially for the loss of their husbands, the Hindústáni women collect their long hair into a braid, called in Sanskrit *veṇi*.

*The mango twig.*] We shall meet with several allusions to this tree as the favourite of Love and the darling of the bees.

---

## CANTO THIRD.

*Who angers thee,* &c.] To understand properly this speech of Káma, it is necessary to be acquainted with some of the Hindú notions regarding a future state. "The highest kind of happiness is absorption into the divine essence, or the return of that portion of spirit which is combined with the attributes of humanity to its original source. This happiness, according to the philosopher, is to be obtained only by the most perfect abstraction from the world and freedom from passion, even while in a state of terrestrial existence...... Besides this ultimate felicity, the Hindús have several minor degrees of happiness, amongst which is the enjoyment of Indra's Swarga, or, in fact, of a Muhammadan Paradise. The degree and duration of the pleasures of this paradise are proportioned to the merits of those admitted to it; and they who have enjoyed this lofty region of Swarga, but whose virtue is exhausted, revisit the habitation of mortals."—Prof. Wilson's *Megha Dúta.* Compare also "The Lord's Song."—*Specimens of Old Indian Poetry,* pp. 67, 68.

Indra, therefore, may be supposed to feel jealous whenever a human being aspires to something higher than that heaven of which he is the Lord.

The "chain of birth" alluded to is of course the metempsychosis, or transmigration of souls, a belief which is not to be looked upon (says Prof. Wilson in the preface to his edition of the *Sánkhya Káriká*) as a mere popular superstition. It is the main principle of all Hindú metaphysics; it is the foundation of all Hindú philosophy. The great object of their philosophical research in every system, Brahminical or Buddhist, is the discovery of the means of putting a stop to further transmigration; the discontinuance of corporeal being; the liberation of soul from body.

*As on that Snake.*] Sesha, the Serpent King, is in the Hindú mythology the supporter of the earth, as, in one of the fictions of the Edda,—

> " That sea-snake, tremendous curled,
> Whose monstrous circle girds the world."

He is also the couch and canopy of the God Vishṇu, or, as he is here called, Krishṇa,—that hero being one of his incarnations, and considered identical with the deity himself.

*The threefold world.*] Earth, heaven, and hell.

*His fearful Rati.*] The wife of Káma, or Love.

*To where Kuvera, &c.*] The demi-god Kuvera was regent of the north.

*Nor waited for the maiden's touch.*] Referring to the Hindú notion that the Aśoka blossoms at the touch of a woman's foot. So Shelley says,

> " I doubt not, the flowers of that garden sweet
> Rejoiced in the sound of her gentle feet."
>
> *Sensitive Plant.*

*Grouping the syllables.*] This comparison seems forced rather too far to suit a European taste. Kálidás is not satisfied with calling the mango-spray the Arrow of Love; he must tell us that its leaves are the feathers, and that the bees have marked it with the owner's name.

*That loveliest flower.*] The Karnikára.

*His flowery Tilaka.*] The name of a tree; it also means a mark made with coloured earths or unguents upon the forehead and between the eyebrows, either as an ornament or a sectarial distinction; the poet intends the word to convey both ideas at once here. In this passage is another comparison of the mango-spray: it is called the *lip* of Love; its *rouge* is the blush of morning, and its darker beautifying powder the clustering bees. From the universal custom of dying the lips,

H

the Sanskrit poets are constantly speaking of their "vermeil tints," &c., as will be sufficiently evident in the course of this work.

*The Hermit's servant.*] By name Nandi.

*His neck of brightly-beaming blue.*] An ancient legend tells us that after the deluge the ocean was churned by Gods and demons, in order to recover the Amrit and other treasures that had been lost in it:—

> " Then loud and long a joyous sound
>   Rang through the startled sky :
> ' Hail to the Amrit, lost and found ! '
>   A thousand voices cry.
> But from the wondrous churning streamed
>   A poison fierce and dread,
> Burning like fire ; where'er it streamed
>   Thick noisome mists were spread.
> The wasting venom onwards went,
>   And filled the Worlds with fear,
> Till Brahmá to their misery bent
>   His gracious pitying ear ;
> And Śiva those destroying streams
>   Drank up at Brahmá's beck.
> Still in thy throat the dark flood gleams,
>   God of the azure neck ! "
>
> Specimens of Old Indian Poetry—*Churning of the Ocean.*

*Gates of sense.*] The eyes, ears, &c.

---

## CANTO FOURTH.

*Late, dim, and joyless shall his rising be.*] The Moon, in Hindú mythology, is a male deity.

*This line of bees.*] Káma's bow is sometimes represented as strung in this extraordinary manner.

*And stain this foot.*] "Staining the soles of the feet with a red colour, derived from the Mehndee, the Lac, &c., is a favourite practice of the Hindú toilet."—WILSON.

## CANTO FIFTH.

*And worn with resting on her rosary.*] The Hindús use their rosaries much as we do, carrying them in their hands or on their wrists. As they turn them over, they repeat an inaudible prayer, or the name of the particular deity they worship, as Vishṇu or S'iva. The *Rudrákshá málá* (which we may suppose Umá to have used) is a string of the seeds or berries of the Eleocarpus, and especially dedicated to S'iva. It should contain 108 berries or beads, each of which is fingered with the mental repetition of one of S'iva's 108 appellations.

*Not e'en her boy.*] Kártikeya, the God of War.

*Of those poor birds.*] The Chakraváki. These birds are always observed to fly in pairs during the day, but are supposed to remain separate during the night.

*That friendship soon in gentle heart is bred.*]
"Amor in cor gentil ratto s'apprende."
DANTE.

## CANTO SIXTH.

*The Heavenly Dame.*] Arundhatí, wife of one of the Seven Saints.

*The Boar.*] An Avatár, or incarnation of Vishṇu. In this form he preserved the world at the deluge.

*That thirsty bird.*] The Chátaka, supposed to drink nothing but rain-water.

*Proud Alaká.*] The capital of Kuvera, the God of Wealth.

*The bright Champac.*]
"The maid of India blest again to hold
In her broad lap the Champac's leaves of gold."
*Lalla Rookh.*

*Angiras.*] One of the Seven Saints; the father of Vrihaspati, the teacher of the gods.

*Vast grew his body.*] Alluding to the Vámana, or Dwarf Avatár of Vishṇu, wrought to restrain the pride of the giant Bali, who had expelled the Gods from heaven. In that form he presented himself before the giant, and asked him for three paces of land to build a hut. Bali ridiculed and granted the request. The dwarf immediately grew to a prodigious size, so that he measured the earth with one pace, and the heavens with another.

*Sumeru.*] Another name of the sacred Mount Meru; or rather the same word, with *su*, good, prefixed.

## CANTO SEVENTH.

*Kailása's side.*] A mountain, the fabulous residence of Kuvera, and favourite haunt of S´iva, placed by the Hindús among the Himálayas.

*Kálí came behind.*] The name of one of the divine matrons. The word also signifies in Sanskrit a row or succession of clouds, suggesting the comparison which follows.

*In twofold language.*] In Sanskrit and Prakrit. The latter is a softened modification of the former, to which it bears the same relation as Italian to Latin; it is spoken by the female characters of the Hindú drama.

THE END.

www.ingramcontent.com/pod-product-compliance
Lightning Source LLC
Chambersburg PA
CBHW022127160426
43197CB00009B/1176